MW00437612

Walk In My Boots ~
The Joy of Connecting

*Make every
Connection
Count!*

Bonnie

By
Bonnie Ross-Parker

Walk in My Boots ~ The Joy of Connecting
by Bonnie Ross-Parker

Editor: Barbara McNichol
Cover Design: Bookcovers.com
Book Design: Paula Chance
Copyright ©2003

All rights reserved.
No portion of this book may be reproduced in any form
without written permission from the publisher.

Lilli Publishing, LLC

For more information, contact:
Bonnie Ross-Parker
www.bonnierossparker.com

ISBN: 0-9724061-0-7 Paperback
ISBN: 0-9724061-1-5 Adobe Reader EBook
ISBN: 0-9724061-2-3 Microsoft Reader EBook

Library of Congress Cataloging-in-Publication Data has been applied for.

FOREWORD

As I read *Walk in My Boots~The Joy of Connecting*, a feeling of joy was ever-present. I could *"hear"* Bonnie as she shared her journey. I found her voice to be soothing, encouraging, supportive and heartfelt.

While there are many lessons available, the essence of this book is that she beautifully and poignantly tells her story. She allows us to absorb the insights that apply rather than tell us what we *have* to do.

Connection is not some topic Bonnie decided to write about . . . it's her way of life! She did not have to rely on research. She *lives* the concepts she shares with her reader. The book flows from chapter to chapter in a logical, instructive and easy to follow format which nourishes, enlightens and inspires.

Whether it is her connection to self, family, community, colleagues or to values, Bonnie tells her truth in a loving, open manner, overflowing from her heart into ours.

— *Susan RoAne*
Keynote Speaker,
Best-selling Author of *How to Work a Room*

DEDICATION

I dedicate this book to honor my mother, Lillian Clark Renert, who through her own selfless example, taught me the the joy of connecting. With untiring commitment, unwavering support and love, she has touched the lives of hundreds and hundreds of people with her generosity. Her caring spirit continues to be a beacon of light to all who know her. She gives and gives and the universe continues to reward her with wonderful friends, a devoted family, and a loving husband, Robert, who has shared his life with her for over 60 years. Thank you for my life and for the gift of having you as my mom. I love you.

TRIBUTE

Additionally, I honor my father, Robert Reuben Renert, for being in his own quiet way, not only a huge champion for my mom, but a wonderful example of a gentle, loving soul. A devoted husband and committed family man, he has continuously and without reservation expressed his love both verbally and affectionately. We laugh at his jokes and appreciate his quick sense of humor. He has significantly impacted the lives of all who know him. I love you.

TABLE OF CONTENTS

10% of all profits from the sale of *Walk In My Boots* will be donated to further research
for Ehlers-Danlos Syndrome Type IV through the Ehlers-Danlos National Foundation
(www.ednf.org), and The Department of Pathology at Washington State University
(www.wsu.edu) as well as for other related projects.

Section 6: Cultivating Community Connections

Section 7: Connecting Through The Red Door

Section 8: Disconnections

Section 9: Re-connecting — with yourself

Section 10: The Joy of Connecting

Those Who Have Connected The Connector (With Gratitude)

Because connecting is such an integral part of my life, it's challenging to call to mind times I wasn't doing what I do so naturally now. I can't recall a "beginning" to it all or a defining moment. It's a process that I've developed over the years, experienced its effectiveness, and shared with others.

Connecting is taking time to listen beyond hearing, to care beyond superficiality, and to share gifts with others. My life has evolved through the genuine giving of individuals who have been connectors for me. They have blessed me with their generous spirits, their unwavering faith, ideas, resources, and experiences that have filled me up to overflowing.

These people are an important part of my story and deserve recognition.

Mardeene Mitchell and I met through a networking event. When I first decided to write my book, I asked her to be my writing coach. Before saying "yes," she asked to review some of my earlier writings to decide whether she'd be interested in taking on my project. When she agreed to help me, I was thrilled. Our experience together — and her relentless requests for me to "dig deeper" and "search my soul" — provided me with huge opportunities for personal growth. It was her belief in me that inspired me to create something bigger than I might otherwise have imagined.

Barbara Keddy and I share a long-standing friendship that began through franchising. When I need a resource or idea, I can count on Barbara getting back to me with an answer to my request. She's cheered my high times, encouraged me during my low times, and has been an unwavering, non-judgmental friend. When I decided to develop this book, Barbara was with me from the beginning and throughout the process. The President of Be Great! Marketing, she is my co-creator as I share my message via the internet.

Dawn Billings is the woman I've counted on day or night, who has counseled me and taken me from upside down to right side up. Dawn guides me through my emotional states and gets me to think clearly and act appropriately. She refuses to "let me off the hook" when I get overwhelmed. I can count on Dawn to walk me through the fog into the sunshine. She is an amazing listener, processor, and friend who continues to shower me with her generosity. Many of my lessons about the joy of gratitude I've learned through her example. Her book *Entitled To Fail: Endowed To Succeed* testifies to the difference we can make when we focus on appreciation as a way of life. She lives her lessons every day. I am one of her greatest admirers.

Linda Larsen and I met at a National Speakers Association convention. During one of the sessions, she gave me a copy of her book *True Power*. That gift has had a significant impact on my life. I've read it many times over and recommended it to friends. I've been the recipient of her ideas and support ever since. There's something about Linda that invites openness — you just know she sincerely cares about you. I feel certain she's proud of me for carrying out my vision through this book.

Dr. Jill Kahn is my Spiritual Healer. Although I went to her for chiropractic care, she offered me much, much more. Getting Jill's help at times of crisis turned the tide. Over time and through our sessions, I increased my understanding of life choices and clarified my journey's purpose. I went from feeling depleted to feeling fulfilled. Through Jill, I learned it was not only all right to ask for what I needed, but it was healthy to do so. *The Gift of Taking*, which Jill wrote, has inspired my own work. I lovingly refer to her as Dr. Jill — an unwavering source of strength in my life.

Sandra Yancey, CEO of eWomenNetwork, Inc., has shared the value of visionary thinking with me. I've learned many lessons from Sandra, a woman of steadfast focus and sheer determination, who started a women's website by building a membership community of women. Sandra and I have exchanged ideas, weathered storms, and come out stronger than before as individuals. Through her example, I clearly see what can be achieved when one gets committed.

Mary Foley is the author of *Bodacious*. When I read that book, I became determined to meet this incredible woman and I did! In many ways her insights fueled me with the power to stand up for what I believe and to show by example the value of strength and courage. Mary's the kind of friend I can call anytime for help. She's great at offering a solid opinion when asked, helping others through self-discovery, and being a sounding board during times of confusion. She's just so approachable and caring. I count on Mary's authenticity. Her friendship has been a huge source of encouragement in creating my book.

Bruce Berns instilled in me the foundation for where

I am today. When I decided to become the Associate Publisher of *The Gazette*, I had no idea if I was up to the task. The confidence and trust Bruce showed me made the difference. The experience of working with him, the commitment I made to writing, and the connections I forged with women through my column have all come together. In many ways, writing has brought me the fulfillment I experience today. His commitment to what he saw in me never wavered. I am grateful to Bruce for the enduring relationship we created, one that continues to extend beyond our professional lives.

Kirsten Farris has steadfastly remained my intuitive friend, business consultant, and trusted confidant. Through the ups and downs of my professional life, Kirsten offered the insight and clarity I needed to travel the winding roads. In spite of her hectic schedule, Kirsten responded to my every request. Together we created a wonderful mentoring group, which we named The Red Door. The insights she shared with me and the women we mentored have guided us all. I respect Kirsten. I appreciate her. I trust her and the honesty with which she shared her views. While she never told me what to do, I knew that what she advised came from love. Her ideas continue to serve me well.

Barbara McNichol, was the last pair of eyes to review the manuscript. Her wonderful expertise as an editor gave *Walk In My Boots ~ The Joy of Connecting* its final form.

Steve Cohn, my incredible friend, took on the task of sifting through everything I had written and putting it all together to create *Walk In My Boots ~ The Joy of Connecting*. He worked magically with hundreds of pages and hours of interviews to weave them together, bringing clarity and cohesiveness to what I wanted to share. His keen eye and understanding kept the essence of my ideas and the passion of my message intact. He took my heart and captured it in a way that maintained my integrity and style. The tireless effort he put into this book plus his excitement over my project kept me going. He captured what I wanted to say. I am indebted to him for his unwavering friendship and incredible skill.

I am grateful to my children, **Elizabeth** and **Glenn**. I know they've been challenged to understand their mom and the role(s) I play. While I may not always meet with their approval, they have remained supportive. I know they love me. They know I love them. As we each experience our own journeys, we continue to adjust and strengthen and re-define who we are with one another.

Phil, my husband, is first, foremost, and forever my most treasured companion. His love sustains me, inspires me, and encourages me. In the years we've shared, he's witnessed my changes, weathered my storms, and remained vigilant in his support. With the writing of this book and in all of my endeavors, he's ever ready and willing to endorse my choices. Ours is and will ever be my deepest, unconditional heart-to-heart connection.

SECTION 1

A Journey of Connection

Walk In My Boots

Connection.

It is a word that I cannot separate from who I am, what I feel, or what I believe. It is a part of my heart, my soul, and my life. It is something that I wake up each day striving for — a connection with others, a connection to the world, a connection with myself.

It's a vital part of everything I do and everything I seek.

"But Bonnie," say those who know me. "It comes so naturally to you. With everything going on in my life, I could never find the joy of connecting that you find every day."

I believe you can. I believe that you already have the ability to connect. With the ability to connect, you have the ability to live a fuller, more successful, more joyous life. All you have to do is take a journey on the road to connecting, as I have.

The Joy of Connecting is really about valuing yourself and shifting your consciousness to share yourself with others. Each time you give someone a compliment or encouragement, or show you value them, you are saying "I recognize you — I connect with you. You are important."

It's really easy to go the extra mile when you are happy and connected with yourself. It's joyful to want others to feel good about themselves. In the uncertain world of today, we need to belong more than ever.

We need to connect.

Many people live in a sad place right now. People everywhere are hurting. Connection offers a feeling of belonging.

It's really simple. You can brighten someone's day just

by saying, "Hello." You can acknowledge someone through your smile. Just bring who you are to wherever you are and connect in some way.

None of us can escape the harried and uncertain circumstances we live in. We are more aware than ever before of the fragility of life and the impact of the threat of terrorism. We can remain isolated, disconnected, and frightened of the unknown, or we can create connections and relationships that strengthen, support, honor, love, and enrich us. The choice is ours to make. We are all connected as part of the human family. Why not live the connection!

It's not difficult. It's not stressful. It's not even physical. The journey to connect can start today for you as it started for me so many years ago.

Why Did I Write This Book?

If you are holding this book in your hands, there is a good chance you have attended one of my Joy of Connecting groups or seminars, know somebody who has, or heard about somebody who has. Perhaps you have been doing some connecting yourself or would like to do more.

Seeing the hundreds of people I meet each year, I have observed that a lot of people go about their daily tasks on automatic pilot. They really don't take the time to consider or recognize or even focus on how their behavior, both verbal and non-verbal, affects other people. So I decided to write a book that represents a journey to get individuals — particularly women — to think about the impact they can have on their community by offering their gifts and talents to others. Perhaps with this book, I can even facilitate a caring attitude and be a conduit for a more loving world.

The book is designed to create a story in which the reader looks at her own specialness and brings who she is to her connections. As with all ways of connecting, this brings value to both the receiver and the giver.

The book's concept — *Walk In My Boots* — is an invitation to walk beside me and be inspired by the stories and ideas shared here. I see this book as a journey, a pathway to expanded awareness about one's self, how we can relate to each other more effectively, and how we can increase the joy that comes from honoring and growing our relationships.

This book is made up of 10 sections, each addressing a way of connecting. Every section begins with a story from my life, followed by ideas, stories, essays, and sometimes poetry that link to the section's topic. I hope that by reading these pieces, you will be warmed, touched, inspired, and challenged to make connecting a way of life.

People Want to Connect

I think today there is so much that distances us from each other. We are a society of individuals who are so busy, so stressed, so overloaded, and so fragile, we don't make the time to connect.

Yet I believe as people, we want to connect — need to connect. We need to feel part *of*, not apart *from* each other. We go about our daily tasks and struggle to balance home life and work. If only we could recognize the joy that we can experience by taking even small moments of time to connect — a quick exchange, a handwritten note acknowledging someone who serves you, a compliment, or a conversation during waiting time.

These are all avenues for connecting. Both parties

benefit, and it sets "connecting" in motion! We can enrich each other even in small, seemingly insignificant ways. It takes willingness to do so. It means being conscious and conscientious. It means taking the lead. It means feeling positive about yourself and wanting to share that "positivity."

Connections create joy. So let's be inspired by the joy we can experience together.

Why the Title *Walk in My Boots?*

I collect cowboy boots. The concept of Walk in My Boots is similar to the saying "walk in my shoes." It represents a shared venture.

Walking is energetic. It's invigorating. When we walk, we connect with our bodies and the environment. For me, walking takes me out of the routine and brings me into natural daylight — beauty, sounds, aromas. By journeying together, we enrich our understandings, try something new, and get in step with each other. By walking together, we can exchange our ideas enroute. *The Joy of Connecting* is the writer and reader connecting by sharing experiences.

"Connecting" is my life passion. I feel most alive when I am connecting. It doesn't matter where I am — inviting a conversation in the dentist's office, waiting in line at the post office or check-out counter, or chatting with a server at a restaurant. People fascinate me. I derive tremendous joy in finding out more about someone, in evoking a smile, in expressing appreciation. I experience a natural magical high when I engage someone in a conversation.

Connecting is my way of bringing a smile, letting someone feel noticed and valued, offering friendship, and lightening up what otherwise might be a mundane experience. (After all, who likes waiting in line?)

For example, I habitually thank people who support me by using words they're not expecting. Instead of saying "Thank you," which we usually express automatically and without thought, I like to say, "I appreciate you." Same message — different words heard in a way that lingers with the recipient. And it usually evokes a "Thank you" back! To me, telling others I appreciate them is a real connection.

Many individuals enhance and assist us, yet we rarely take the time to express appreciation for their contribution. Perhaps it's because we don't feel as good about ourselves as we should. That can happen when people don't connect with each other.

Here's the vicious cycle. First, people don't show appreciation to each other. Then the people who should be appreciated don't feel that they are, and therefore do not feel good about themselves. When they don't feel good about themselves, they don't tell others how much they appreciate what they do. End result: it's easy to take one another for granted.

The answer? I believe when people feel good about themselves, it's natural to want others to feel good about themselves as well. The joy of connecting brings value to each party involved. While it takes little effort to appreciate others, the dividends are huge. You have better relationships. You have better and more caring friends. You feel more productive and more a part of something bigger than yourself. Hey! Even your love life will be better!

I truly think individuals would do more for themselves and others if they thought people really appreciated them. So let's do more to acknowledge others. All it takes is a slight shift in behavior to expand who we are and encourage others to do the same.

It's my singular mission to spread good cheer wherever I go. I want to create a ripple effect that travels around the world.

The Days I Walked

This book joyously shares my tale of walking in the Avon 3-Day Walk in Georgia to eliminate breast cancer. For three days in October 2001, I put myself on the line — physically, mentally, and spiritually — with 3,000 other participants. We walked to honor all the women who have had, or one day will have, breast cancer.

I walked for two friends who were then dealing with breast cancer — Deb Haggerty and Marcia Steele. The knowledge that I was walking for them — connecting with them — gave me the strength and the push to do what I needed to do. Deb and Marcia's spirits carried me along through the physical (training) and the mental (believing in myself and the cause) aspects. My connection with them helped me commit to and work toward honoring my commitment throughout the fund raising required.

What a wonderful thing it was to share the experience of the walk with all of the other participants. How wonderful to know that by doing this, I was not only helping Deb and Marcia, but also contributing to the greater cause — raising awareness and helping women globally — contributing to the global heart.

This is what connection does. In the end, "I did it." I prepared. I crossed the finish line. I did what I set out to do. The connections were all there.

In a way it was a singular accomplishment, though I walked for 60 miles with 3,000 others. I had to do everything possible on my own to complete what I set out to do.

Other people were looking to me to see if I would carry out my responsibility. They had put their faith, confidence and money in me. In return, I was there for them. I was prepared. I connected with myself on all levels *first*, and then brought my *whole* self to the journey.

We walked as individuals. We shared the experience. We supported and encouraged each other along the way. It was a journey of connection from the beginning until the end.

As a collective community, we make a huge impact. But like any community, we serve best when we bring our best forward. The Avon Walk represented our best individual efforts as a collective voice. Peace, awareness, determination, healing. We can't do individually what we can do collectively. That is the lesson!

Connecting Even Though the World Stands in Our Way

I taught 6th grade for 12 years. Although I haven't been in the classroom for several years, I recently began thinking about my classroom setting and how the world got in the way.

During the first several years of my teaching career, I created a relaxed environment. I loved my students. I loved teaching. My students could count on me to talk with, to be hugged, and to be encouraged. My school district was lower/middle class and families having two-income earners in the household was the norm. Single parenting was also common. Over time, however, certain restrictions were placed on all of us. We were told to never be alone in a classroom with a student. There was to be no physical contact between teacher and student, no matter how young. For someone who is both spontaneous and affectionate, this mandate was difficult to adhere to. My students needed affection. Our success together was in part due to the hugs of support that I delivered and they knew they could count on. Verbal connection remained, however, the physical hugs, tousling of hair, quick shoulder squeezes had to stop. All of a sudden, the easygoing atmosphere was replaced by distance and disconnection. I felt restricted. It just wasn't the same.

It's frightening to think that due to a few incidents of physical abuse, every classroom teacher became suspect and confined. I suddenly felt on guard, making certain I didn't do or say anything that could be misunderstood or misinterpreted. Preparing each day for the classroom was coupled with caution. Every teacher had to be very careful in all areas of behavior. Consequently, we all lost out.

The way I view it, teachers have a large influence on the children they teach. To have to exhibit behavior that is distanced and guarded, especially during a child's younger years, sends a wrong message! Children not only need to feel good about themselves, they also need to appreciate adults and each other.

One of the lessons our schools are supposed to teach is how to exhibit appropriate behavior. Yet affection has been deemed inappropriate. I felt depleted. The effort each day to create lesson plans for over 125 students, showing care and concern for each child, and having to hold back the emotional side of our relationships became very stressful. I left the teaching profession eventually.

Reconnecting with Life

I often wonder how many people feel disconnected in life. We hear examples of it all the time. Perhaps it's been years since we've talked with a particular family member, a former college friend, or a previous neighbor or business colleague. We (myself included) get so caught up in the routines of life that we let time and distance separate us from those with whom we were once lovingly connected.

I suspect this is indicative of most busy, stressed, and overloaded individuals. The nuclear family, as we once experienced it, is a dinosaur. People often move away from the community in which they were raised. Healthy grandparents are living on their own and older parents have retired in communities far from their loved ones. Despite the plethora of books and websites offering to put us in touch with past friends, classmates, neighbors, colleagues, or just past experiences, so many of us feel alone.

While I recognize that our circumstances change, sending out a communication at holiday time, for birthdays, or for no occasion at all is better than disconnecting altogether. Instead of focusing on how much we've become disconnected, let's begin addressing ways to connect again.

Often, to become connected, we have to rely on new contacts in unfamiliar surroundings. In new settings, it becomes more crucial for us to find ways to connect. If being disconnected is becoming the "acceptable norm," I'm committed to bringing us back to inclusion, caring, support and interdependence. We've become a technological society. Within that society, we need to become a more connected community.

This book speaks to the value of connections and encourages you to take steps to re-connect with others you've known in the past. Its rewards can be enormous.

Connecting Womanhood: The Avon Walk

Deb Haggerty touched my heart. An incredible, vibrant woman from Orlando, Florida, we connected through my husband, Phil. Deb and Phil are both active in the National Speakers Association.

One day I heard her story about her challenge with breast cancer.

When breast cancer came to Deb, it wasn't a surprise. She had always expected it because it ran in her family. Though she was not surprised, she did become angry — angry that so many women get it, angry that the treatment, in some cases, is so invasive. She was 51 years old — in the prime of her life — ten years younger than her mother was when she got cancer.

What do you do when you've just passed 50 and you're faced with a disease that could mean an untimely death at worst, and permanent effects to your body at best? Where do you find courage?

Deb found it through connecting.

Rather than feeling sorry for herself, she demanded to become active in her own care and survival. She asked herself, "OK, so what can I do about this?" She surfed the Internet and soaked up all the information she could. She educated herself on taking control of her own body and her own life. She refused to let it stop her business; she refused to cover her head with a wig or scarves. She felt people needed to see other people dealing with this disease. The only time she made an exception was for her daughter's wedding. She treated herself to a wig.

At the same time I heard another friend, Marcia Steele, had also been diagnosed with breast cancer. So many women, so much pain.

Their stories inspired me. They made me aware through their connections with me. Now I would do my part for them.

I decided that I would honor both Deb and Marcia by walking the Avon 3-Day Walk in October 2001. The Walk would cover 60 miles from Lake Lanier (north of Atlanta) to Piedmont Park in Atlanta. I had seven months to train.

Finding Courage by Connecting

Connecting with others elicits courage. The Chinese philosopher Lao-Tzu said, "To love someone deeply gives you strength. Being loved by someone deeply gives you courage."

I certainly didn't know if I could walk 60 miles. I had never trained for anything like this. I had always stayed in pretty good shape, but this was different. This was a commitment to something else. This was a commitment to other people — people in pain and people in need.

I know I couldn't have done something so outside my everyday life without a compelling reason. Through it all, one thought kept me going. If the courage and strength of these women could keep them going through life, surely I could develop the strength and courage to walk 60 miles to support them.

The more I thought about it, the more I realized that the same way walkers were helping people like Deb and Marcia, others would be there for me. We don't have to go it alone! Support is available for whatever challenge we meet because people *want* to help. They'll always be there if we just look for them.

I chose to help Deb with her healing. At first, she couldn't believe a near-total stranger would do that for her. She helped me push forward and encouraged me to stretch where I had never stretched before. We connected because we cared.

The training began. At first, the going was tough. I had to get used to walking long distances alone. As a life-time connector, the solitude of walking by myself was hard! I began to walk with a tape player or CD player attached to my clothing. As I increased the time and distance I walked, motivational music helped significantly. I worked up to walking three to four hours a day. As I hit my stride, I found myself reaching the 10-mile mark, the 15-mile mark and, eventually, the 20-mile mark. I wore out three pairs of walking shoes!

To keep on track with my training, I walked in the rain. Some days, I came home chilled from the cold or exhausted from the heat. Some days, I took Epsom® salts baths to soothe my tired legs and feet. By the end of the summer, I was walking for five hours, soaking in a tub for one hour, and sleeping for two more. Walking had almost become a full-time job!

I'm certain friends and family thought I was crazy to spend so much time committing to this challenge. Yet, they still supported me both financially and by asking me how I was holding up!

Keeping the Connections in My Heart

At times, dealing with the solitude of training alone became more difficult than almost anything I'd ever done. Day after day, mile after mile, took sheer determination —

not only to do what I said I'd do, but also to be an example of what's possible when one stays focused. I knew when I did it for myself, I was doing it for others. The task lightened as I began to feel pride instead of fatigue. My body got stronger; I lost weight and felt terrific.

Still, despite walking by myself on this journey, my connection with Deb, Marcia, and my purpose assured me that I was never completely alone. That's the secret of connecting.

Through the seven months of training, I kept the spirits of Deb and Marcia in my heart and their faces in my mind. Their determination in confronting cancer kept me pushing forward. How small were my concerns about my tired legs and my stamina compared to what Deb and Marcia had to think about each night? How did they cope as they wondered what was waiting for them the next day?

Every day, I affirmed my success. I listened to motivational songs. I visualized the finish line. I prayed for continued good health, not only during the Walk, but after it as well. I prayed for these two friends. Mostly, I prayed that I would cherish this experience and remember it for how it shaped me as a person.

The Walk Begins

I was ready. It was almost time to leave for Lake Lanier. Deb and I talked the day before. I was thrilled to remind her of her specialness and told her that, throughout the Walk, I would be thinking of her and admiring her courage. She assured me that I'd be fine. As her words entered my heart, I knew I'd made the right decision. I am certain if tables were turned, Deb would be as supportive of me.

The Walk connected me with a grand community of people who care enough to do whatever it takes to make possible what seems impossible. We walked for those who were battling the disease. We walked for those surviving it. We walked for those who had lost the battle. We walked for their loved ones. We walked to show an observant community our solidarity. We walked because we could. We walked because it was the right thing to do. We walked for whatever reasons our hearts demanded of us. And yes, we walked for the world! We knew that walking in our collective "boots" was the path to connecting our global hearts. Of that, I am certain.

As incredible as the preparation had been, nothing could equal the overwhelming emotion of the event itself. Walking side-by-side with the survivors, their friends and loved ones, connecting as sisters with purpose, we spoke freely, cried openly, shared stories, exchanged supplies, encouraged and assisted one another. We had a sense of accomplishment as individuals and as one huge, tired, elated family.

We traveled three consecutive days, from one community to the next, during the heat of the summer. The campsite each evening brightly displayed lights and blue tents against the dark night sky, welcoming 3,000 walkers who dragged themselves in, feeling exhausted and elated. The organizers set up music, food, medical tents, and entertainment. What a feeling to know we were all in this together — connecting with millions of women worldwide so that they would know they're not alone in their struggle. It was worthwhile to know that each and every step each walker made would bring in $40 for cancer education and treatment!

The Finish Line

I recall nearing the end. About one mile from the finish line under the arched sign that read "Welcome to Piedmont Park," I thought I saw my daughter and her family. Could it be? Sure enough, there they were — Liz, Ron, and Eli — waiting for me! When I fell into their hugs, I held on tightly and the tears flowed, celebrating a moment I'll never forget. My dear loves were there for me. I remember thinking how grateful I am to have children in my life who love and honor me. I knew that if I ever had the kind of health challenges some of our walkers faced, my children would remain by my side.

We stepped through the remaining distance together, sometimes holding hands, always smiling, sharing the joy. Not only were we a family connected, we were now connected in this experience as well. It left an indelible impression.

As we crossed the finish line, we saw and heard a sea of faces, clapping hands, loud cheering, happy music, and lots of emotion. Outstretched hands touched us. To be such an integral part of thousands of people whose journeys were forever linked to my own, my heart was touched as never before. As it pumped out of my chest, my spirit connected with the universal spirit. I know now that my contribution — yours, ours — is important to the universal plan. The $8,250 my supporters and I raised contributed to the whole Atlanta fund of $4.4 million!

The closing ceremony for the Walk honored the survivors (those beautiful women in pink shirts and hats) and honored the crew and volunteers who gave unselfishly of their time and expertise, my husband, Phil, among them. When we filed into huge Piedmont Park, there was a sea of cheering well wishers holding balloons, flowers, signs, and kids on shoulders. We all connected for a common cause — to forever eradicate the pain and suffering caused by breast cancer. We were one global family.

After the Walk

My daughter threw a party to celebrate my accomplishment. My husband made up tee-shirts that displayed on one side "The Bonnie Ross-Parker Support Team," and on the other "What I Did For Love." Marcia came to the party, along with other wonderful people who had supported me along the way.

As the months went on, Deb and Marcia miraculously recovered and today are doing well. Like Deb, Marcia was helped by her connections. Friends made a pact to make sure she was never without help for doctor visits, chemotherapy appointments, shopping and more. Marcia's team took care of details and took care of her.

When the doctors told Marcia she was "clean," she was asked what she'd learned from this experience. Marcia, whose work and lifestyle before the cancer had been "driven," pondered the question. Then she said, "I've learned that the most important thing in the world is having friends — people who will love you and care for you and take care of you, no matter what. I don't know what I would have done without all of the people who were there for me."

Connections.

Deb was also thrilled when I told her that I had completed the Walk. The funny thing was that I had decided to walk in her honor even before I'd met her in person. Getting together with her just before the 3-Day Walk was truly an emotional experience. I finally met the woman I'd admired from a distance. She met the mystery woman who'd been walking and walking and walking to support her healing.

We hugged and cried and felt an immediate bond between two spirits. I knew when I looked into her eyes and "saw" her heart that I had made the right decision. Walking 60 miles to help another heal was a small contribution compared to the one Deb was making in my life.

I carried thoughts of Deb with me throughout my training and throughout the 3Day. Our relationship endures because we'll always be part of each other's journey. Our friendship will continue to have meaning and significance.

A Way of Being

Connection is a way of being. We first connect with our own hearts by honoring our individuality, sharing our talents, and caring about others. Only then can we begin the process of offering help and hope to those outside ourselves. Only then can we connect with our community.

When we connect with our community, the ripple effect overflows into the world. We become an integral part of a universal family by offering *our* unique contributions and connecting to the unique contributions of the six billion souls who inhabit this earth. Caring creates a powerful connection and belief. Our connections will one day produce a cure.

Willingness Is A State of Mind

There are endless stories of people we know or read about who achieve whatever they set out to do against seemingly insurmountable odds.

Success is never an overnight occurrence. Entrepreneurs and researchers invest years of time, money, and effort to achieve the results they want. Aspiring movie stars, artists, and musicians practically starve before becoming well known. Many politicians get defeated in numerous campaigns before the public accepts their platforms. Authors describe being rejected over and over before publishers accept their manuscripts.

What separates those who persevere from those who give up? I believe the key is "willingness" — one's willingness to do whatever it takes to reach a goal that ultimately results in what they want.

The journey we travel to make our dreams a reality is irrelevant. What *is* relevant is that the people who reach their goals know that *quitting was never an option!* I suspect that in every situation, one's belief in his or her success outweighed the risks involved.

Willingness is a state of mind. It's being open and receptive to possibilities. It means taking responsibility for the situations and conditions in your life. When you possess a committed attitude, your confidence is elevated. You feel powerful. You feel unstoppable. You are in control. You're willing to pursue your dream regardless of the odds.

If you lived in a perfect world and absolutely *knew* you could eliminate fear and failure, what would you be willing to do to achieve the results you wanted? Perhaps you have a hobby that you've always wanted to pursue as a career. Maybe there's a book inside your head that you need to write. Have you considered returning to school to expand your skills or learn new ones? Do you have a health issue you've been ignoring because the plan of action seemed overwhelming?

Consider how different your life could be if you were willing to take the actions necessary to change its direction! What would success feel like if you were willing to do whatever it takes to get what you want?

The best thing about having an attitude of willingness is that you will find people flocking to you to help on your journey. People like to connect with those who have purpose and direction. Having purpose and direction begins with an attitude of willingness. Let others help you on your journey and your willingness will increase dramatically.

Success is a state of mind. Your willingness to change your mind and change your life is a decision only you can make. Beginning right now, ask yourself this question: What am I willing to do to get what I want?

Finding the Common Denominators

As a former math teacher, it seems to me that the business of connecting with others is about finding the common denominators. It occurs to me that many fractions have common denominators, just as many people share common qualities.

If you don't remember your math lessons (willingly or unwillingly), the numerator of a fraction (the top number) represents its uniqueness. In life, our numerators can represent our differences. What are our differences? The possibilities are endless. We differ in the color of our skin and sound of our voices. We come from diverse cultures, practice different religions, and perform a variety of jobs. We are diverse in the titles we give ourselves and in the roles we perform. Our thoughts and feelings — and the way we express ourselves — are unique to each of us.

When the bottom numbers (the denominator) of fractions are the same, they are called common fractions. While few of us would like to call ourselves "common people," we're similar in many ways to the fraction's denominator.

Just think of all the ways we're similar. We share an unlimited set of values. We all want peace and prosperity, overall good health, love, fulfillment, and meaningful work. We desire a life filled with purpose, safety, lasting relationships, and feelings of self-worth. We need companionship, respect, togetherness, love, and happiness.

Although we're physically different, we share many of the same emotions. It's *who we are inside* that brings us together. Regardless of who we are or where we're from, the common denominator is our desire to create a wonderful and rewarding life.

We're presented with unlimited opportunities to acknowledge each other, to respect each other, to love one another, to honor our differences and do what we can to help each other achieve our individual goals. I can't think of a better way to live. Can you?

Who we are *externally* is our uniqueness. What we share internally is what we have in common.

So Many Combinations

Think of all the different combinations of people in the world. Isn't it amazing? Each person is unique and irreplaceable. Our physical characteristics allow us to see and recognize each other, but it's the uniqueness of the combination of our personal numerators and denominators that make us who we are.

The challenge is to apply this equation to our lives — to apply it to real people and the differences and issues that tend to separate us. If we're spending too much time focusing on our differences rather than our similarities, the solution is to focus on the similarities.

Connecting requires us to do just that. Once we've connected through our "common denominators," we can revel in the joy of our differences.

SECTION 2

Connecting Through Our Legacies

The Beginnings of My Legacy

People say that I do what I do intuitively. To me, doing what I do feels like what I believe it must feel like to be one of God's angels. We're all earth angels when we're doing what we do so well and so passionately.

I always believed I got started on this path of doing for others from watching my own earth angel — my mother, Lillian. I now believe this legacy goes back even further — to my Grandmother Edna.

Mom Tells the Story

When Grandma Edna Clark died in 1961, I was too caught up in my teenage world to really appreciate who she was or her impact on my mom first and, later, on me through my mom. I simply came home from school one day to find out my grandma had died.

There's little around the event I can recall. I didn't have much of a relationship with Grandma Edna. My parents, my two younger brothers, and I would visit her at her tiny apartment. There was little for us to do. She didn't have a TV and we didn't find much pleasure in those visits except for her great cooking. Besides, as a 16 year old, I was too focused on my friends to recognize what an incredible woman she was. In writing this book — and acknowledging the role "connection" has played in my life — I asked my mom questions about my grandmother, my mother's own childhood, and the lessons that shaped who she's become. I know the value I place on connections is huge yet I didn't know where this commitment came from. How did my mom become such an important role model for me? Here's what my mom shared.

She was born in 1923, but the first story she wanted to tell me took place when she was 14. At that time, reversible coats were popular. All her friends had them. One evening, she mustered the courage to ask her father if she could have a new coat. He told her, "If that's what you want, you can have it under one condition. You'll have to earn the money for it." She did. My mom started to work at the age of 14. She traveled quite a distance by bus to work at a variety store. Not only did she earn enough to buy the coat, but also had enough money left over to buy a wrist watch.

My mother's family experience was typical of a family of five children. Her dad, the grandfather I never knew, was born in Russia and came to the United States as a young refugee. He worked hard to support his family after serving in the U.S. Navy as a chief petty officer on a submarine. My mom marveled over the close and loving relationship her parents had — always affectionate, kind, and caring for one another. They felt comfortable showing affection to each other and to their children. Everyone knew how much they loved each other and how devoted they were to their family.

My grandparents met when Grandpa was a recruiting officer for the Navy. He had come to the home of a friend of my grandma's to talk with her friend's brother. My Grandma Edna was visiting at the time. Apparently, he ended up recruiting my grandma! They were married in 1920 when Grandma was 19 — 13 years younger than her 32-year-old groom.

Tragedy Strikes
When my mom was 16, she lived in a third floor

apartment with her parents, 18-year-old sister and three younger brothers aged 13, 11, and 13 months. One day after school, she climbed the three flights to their family's apartment and opened the door to a lot of commotion. She saw several of her mom's friends standing inside. Her father, not knowing he had a heart condition, had suffered a heart attack while climbing the same flight of stairs and died. My grandpa was only 52. My grandma, all of 39 years old, became a widow. My mother and her siblings had to pull together to support their mother and to survive. Caring for their 13-month-old youngest child kept the family going.

My grandfather was not a big money earner. He was a painter/contractor and later became a business agent for the painter's union. He died during the Great Depression and though Grandma did receive a small widow's pension, things weren't easy for the family. Several families offered to adopt the baby, but my grandma would have none of that. My grandma placed him into foster care during the week so she could work while her children were at school. She brought him home on the weekends.

As with most women at the time, Grandma didn't drive while Grandpa was alive. Once he was gone, she decided to get her license. Grandma took to driving almost immediately and named the family car "Bertha" after her own mother. Being able to drive and having a car was a god-send in those days after my grandfather's death. Despite the high cost of gasoline, the family enjoyed the mobility.

Still relatively young, Grandma went back to school to train to be a practical nurse. When the word got out what a wonderful baby nurse she was, her services were in big demand. She would take care of newborns, teach new moms how to care for their babies, and stay with children when their parents went out or traveled on vacation.

Life was very challenging for my Grandma. After losing a husband and raising her children all by herself, tragedy befell the family again when my mom's brother Arthur was a high school junior.

After he suffered a bad fall during a basketball game, doctors discovered he had cancer. Grandma had no insurance and limited funds, but because she was well connected, she had cultivated a relationship with an orthopedic doctor who turned out to be a huge blessing. He made all the arrangements for Arthur to be treated at the Sloan Kettering Cancer Institute in New York. Arthur had two surgeries and a leg amputated, but to no avail. He died in 1942, the year my mom married my dad. Arthur was only 18.

Even though all of this happened more than 40 years ago, my mother tells me that, to this day, women she knows in her hometown of Hartford, Connecticut, talk with great affection about Mrs. Edna Clark.

In spite of her difficult circumstances, my grandmother was admired for her courage and known for her generous spirit, willingness to help out, and positive outlook — the epitome of connection. She helped everyone when she could. She took care of the families who hired her as well as their children's families. Her clients became her friends. She participated in community work when time allowed. She was popular, well known by doctors, and generous in spite of her limited resources.

A Love Story

My mom and dad met on a blind date the day after Valentine's Day in 1942. She was 19; he was 29. (Those

Clark girls liked older men!) Like many in those days, theirs was a whirlwind romance. With World War II raging, nobody knew what tomorrow would bring. In most cases, the only thing young lovers knew was that if a male wasn't currently in the service, he would be soon.

Mom and Dad became engaged in August 1942 and married in October that same year. They lived with Dad's mother to save money and traveled by train to New York City for their honeymoon. Three weeks after their honeymoon, my father was drafted and got stationed in Atlanta.

When arrangements could finally be made, my mom took a 25-hour train ride to Atlanta to join him. It was her first time away from Hartford, on her own, and alone. She didn't even recognize my dad with his "military look" when she met him at the station. They lived in modest quarters for a year and a half. During that time, she became pregnant with me. In 1944, she went back to Hartford to stay with her mom. I was born in November and my father came home the following spring.

An Amazing Woman

My mom is an incredible woman. Connecting with people comes naturally to her. She connects *everywhere*. Perhaps living as one of five children in a house with a widowed mother, she learned the lessons of keeping people together. She also learned to create loving relationships that last a long time.

In many ways, I think my mother got cheated during her teen years. She didn't have the freedom and flexibility that other teenagers had because of her commitment to help her mom and share in the household responsibilities. She rarely had time to enjoy the fun activities of high school but made the best of her situation and learned the value of staying connected.

In her 80+ years, my mom has become street smart. She's a bright woman who has an uncanny sense of reading people. She's extremely observant and knows a lot about life and living. Yet, while she wants to help others in the world, she understands her priorities. Her life revolves around her family, both her own and our extended family. She is devoted to my dad — her partner of 60 years — and to my brothers and me. She dotes on our families. Most importantly, she has remained unwavering in what she values. Family first. No compromise.

A High Standard for Being Human

By her own example, Mom has taught me the value of relationships, of caring, and of connecting. She *helps* people along their journeys, doing whatever she can do to make others feel special. She introduces people to others they need to meet. She acknowledges birthdays and anniversaries, makes phone calls to congratulate or cheer someone, offers transportation when needed, comforts a widow, and finds excuses to help people all the time. She's the first to send a card or gift, give a contribution, call during illness, visit a house of mourning, or offer friendship. I don't know anyone who has done more for more people than my mom. Loved and admired, she sets a high standard for being human.

I recall times when I was younger that I didn't appreciate my mom's way of operating. I found it annoying and intrusive — always "looking out for everyone else." Wherever we'd go, she'd immediately strike up a conversation with a stranger. This happened while traveling, in the elevator, in line at the movies, at the supermarket, even in the waiting room of a doctor's office.

Later in life, I'd call her to find out "what's going on" and she'd be telling me about all the people she knew and what they were doing. "Oh, so and so's daughter just got married." Or "Do you remember so and so from your high school class? Well, guess what? He just landed a fabulous job with whomever." I can't count the times she'd call me and begin a new story with, "You'll never guess who I met today!" No doubt as my daughter, Elizabeth reads this, she's going to immediately identify *my* behavior with that of my mom's.

Mom is not an involved and complex woman. She simply gets engaged in life. Born, raised, and still living in Hartford during the summer months, and Florida during the winter season, my mom knows everyone and they know her!

No one can forget her, she's so *present* wherever she is. She participates, orchestrates, and demonstrates her capacity to love and to care every day. She just *knows* when others need help and is quick to respond to the call.

To know her is to respect and love her.

From Generation to Generation

Throughout the years, my mom continues to feel proud that she's the daughter of "the late Mrs. Clark," my Grandmother Edna. I believe her generous spirit, caring behavior, and eagerness to connect with others comes from what my grandmother modeled for her.

She talks about her own mom with much love and admiration, saying, "Your grandmother could make a nickel out of a penny. She knew how to stretch every resource she had. She knew how to give in immeasurable ways." Knowing about the woman who raised her, it's no surprise to me that my mom is an amazing woman who gives love unconditionally. She could have been brought up in a home filled with anger and bitterness because of the circumstances they faced. Instead, Grandma kept the family together, treated everyone with love, and left a legacy of which she could be proud. Both of them have passed down the lessons of caring from one generation to the next — lessons I hope I've passed on to my children as well.

I've learned the skills she practices and admired the ease with which she relates to others. Clearly, I have patterned my behavior after hers. What a realization. No wonder I love her so much! What I see in her, others see in me. Surprise!

The relationships I have with my mom and dad have come full circle, influencing the relationship I have with my husband, Phil. Because both of his parents are deceased, Phil has strongly gravitated toward mine. He lovingly accepts them, willingly listens to my mom's stories over and over, and recognizes her strong and endearing qualities. He benefits from her affectionate nature and values her wisdom.

My folks are the old-fashioned kind of parents. The marriage my mom and dad enjoy unquestionably reflects their unwavering and unconditional love for each other. Despite their limited educations, they've built a solid family, created financial security, and generously given their time and resources to others. Phil shares my tremendous respect for them.

A Dedication to Lillian

My mom Lillian is the most generous person I know. Her example has set the stage for me, and I am grateful for it. By her "doing the right thing" in the way she lives her life, I have become that person, too.

If you read the opening pages of this book (so many people skip them so they can get right into the good stuff!), you would have seen that I dedicated this book to my mother. The more I worked on the idea of writing *Walk In My Boots*, the more I realized how natural it was to dedicate it to the person who taught me most about connections. I walk in *her* shoes.

During all the years I've observed my mom, she has shown me the importance of being a good and kind person. It's not just what my mother does that matters. It's who she is.

This book — and the whole idea of connecting — reflects that for connecting to bring us all we desire and need, it has to come from inside. Yes, my mom cares about people and supports them. She's clearly loved not only for what she *does* but for who she *is*. She was a "networker" years ago before anybody knew what that meant and she continues to be "a connector." My mother is "out there," and is interested in meeting new people.

Mom has shown me by her example what to value. I could never repay her for the huge contribution she's made in my life. She's a great lady and a wonderful role model. I love my mom and honor the enormous positive influence she's had on my life.

Today, I'm in a position to honor what she has done to support me, my family, and my life. I see this book as a living testimonial to the woman who exemplifies the power of caring through connection. It represents a tangible way I can express my appreciation to her. It's a legacy of love we can share forever.

Our Contributions

Sometimes when I get caught up learning about famous people and their accomplishments, I begin to wonder about the worth of my own contribution to the world. I can affirm my value as a daughter, wife, mother, grandmother, sister, friend, community volunteer, and writer. I know that through those efforts, I "make a difference." However, I wonder what someone has to do create either "legacy" or "notoriety."

Legacy refers to "something received from the past," usually handed down from one generation to another. We refer to people of notoriety as those who are "generally known or talked about." They receive wide recognition because of their deeds or actions. I love the concept of leaving a legacy. I'm not sure about the idea of being notorious!

As women, we influence our families and communities in so many unselfish ways. Collectively, we possess a strong commitment to social change, health and well-being, and the environment.

Connecting with ourselves and creating who we wish to be is a vital part of the joy of connecting that connects us with others. Each person, each connection, and each time you touch somebody else leaves a legacy to the world. Just as my grandmother influenced her mother, she has left a legacy to me and I am leaving a legacy to my children.

I once heard someone say, "Who you are is the direct result of everything that has ever happened to you, everything you have ever done, and every person you have ever met to this point in your life." What a powerful statement. The reality is even more powerful.

"Who you are" stems from all the things mentioned

above. It comes from those in past generations who influenced those who have influenced you in your life. The legacies we leave create an immortality that will influence generations to come — long after we are gone and forgotten.

Think of the people who have made an impact on your life. Who are they? Why have they influenced you so greatly? What do you admire about the way they lived their lives? What is your own unique contribution?

I think of women who have influenced my life because of the difference they've made. Mother Teresa, Helen Keller, and Anne Frank come to mind. We know the stories of these three women — poverty, severe handicaps, and incredible courage during danger and hardship. All were congruent with their life purpose. By holding true to themselves and being of service to others, they each left an indelible imprint for all eternity. Their legacies have touched people they never could have imagined touching.

I don't anticipate reaching the stature of any of these women, but I do know that I'm offering the world what I believe to be true. By example, I am creating a community through which connection is valued, appreciated, and operative.

Mother Teresa, Helen Keller, and Anne Frank *connected* us to their lives and to their beliefs. They opened the window to improved understanding, to greater concern for fellow travelers, and to faith. They didn't enlighten the world only for themselves. They gave that we might become enlightened, too.

Be the Change You Want to See in the World!

For a long time, my friend Barbara Gulesserian held a vision of establishing a Women's Center — a physical space where women of different backgrounds and generations could come together to learn, to support, to share, to be inspired, to take classes, and to participate.

Initially, the "Center" was held in various women's homes. At one point, the owner of a beautiful art gallery offered her space after hours for the Center's gatherings. Today, the officially named "The Sharing Center for Women—*Where Generations Connect*" has now opened in its own space in Norcross, Ga.

With Donya Robinson as its Executive Director, The Center is a connecting point providing services to enrich and enhance women's lives while creating a sense of community. Through its mentoring, teaching, healing and support services, the Center connects talented women with girls and women of all ages. It's also a central clearinghouse for programs and services offered within the community. Its vision is to help and connect women and girls across all generations, ethnic origins, classes, physical conditions, spiritual beliefs, and sexual identities.

What Are You Leaving as Your Legacy?

Are you aware of the difference you make in the grand scheme of life?

To determine your legacy, take time to discover and acknowledge the good in yourself and in others. It is one of the major reasons I enjoy what I do. I see the good possibilities in people and encourage them to go for the brass ring of their dreams.

My friend Suzanne, President of Sleep-to-Dream, shows what's possible when we receive encouragement. Although she works as a bartender to pay her bills, she is a total entrepreneurial spirit. Having developed an innovative gift line of high end potpourri "dream pillows" and small silk evening bags, she's marketing them to hotel chains, spas, specialty shops, and corporations as unique gifts. Sure, she gets discouraged at times, but she refuses to quit. She knows she has a great product.

Suzanne believes in herself and her creativity. When a big break comes her way, watch out!

There have been days when nothing seemed to go her way. I've reminded her that her hard work will pay off. She has borrowed my belief, held it close, and persevered. It's not a matter of "if" she will live her dream; it's only a matter of "when."

Connect to Care

We are each given the gift of bringing who we are to the world.

We can't become for one another what we don't accept for ourselves as truth. I believe my legacy is to enlighten others to recognize that *connection is joy*. What is yours?

Recognizing all that we do is cause for celebration! We can teach what we value. We can lead by example. We can guide, encourage, and acknowledge. We can love. As each of us contributes who we are to the world, we are both creating and leaving our legacies. The difference we make today and tomorrow sparks its own ripple effect. That effect over time is what we leave behind and for which we are remembered.

Actively participating in each other's journeys and supporting our individual contributions is how we can contribute to each other's success. When we care, we connect. We connect when we care. They are one.

SECTION 3

Primary Connections

Our Family Connections

My first marriage occurred during my senior year of college. I married my high school sweetheart. It was 1965 and the Vietnam War was raging. The great fear for us, as with many young couples, was my husband getting drafted.

Irv and I had been married for a little over a year. I was finishing my studies and he was preparing for the CPA exam. One day we received a letter from the Hartford draft board with information regarding his reporting for a physical in Hartford. At that point we were living in the Washington DC area. Irv wrote to request a change of place for his physical and ended up reporting to a draft board in Richmond, Virginia. While waiting for his induction notice, he made a decision to explore options including Officers Candidate School and the Reserves. Both had no openings. As luck would have it, the unexpected happened. I became pregnant. The Hartford draft board was not enlisting fathers or expectant fathers. Along with joy and love, our beautiful baby girl, Elizabeth, brought safety for her dad.

Elizabeth was born with a gorgeous head of black hair, flawless skin, and an outgoing personality. We took her anywhere and everywhere. Although at age 22 I felt ill prepared for parenting, I found myself to be a natural mom. I had learned how to sew, so I made her lots of dresses and jumpers. Elizabeth was one well-dressed child! As a toddler, she wore a jersey, leggings, and a matching jumper or a dress most of the time. Everybody knew when Elizabeth was around. They could spot her by her fashions!

From the beginning of motherhood, I had so much fun taking care of Elizabeth. We'd play, go to the children's hour at the library, and spend time with other young mothers in a "babysitting co-op". The way we as young mothers worked together was an early model of "connection".

Our family occupied a modest home in a modest neighborhood in suburban Virginia and most of our neighbors were also parenting young children. Elizabeth had lots of toddlers with whom to play. Because both of our families were living in Hartford, I leaned on other mothers for help. We all supported one another.

Glenn Is Born

Not unlike any other mother expecting another child, I struggled when I became pregnant for the second time. I couldn't imagine I could love another child as much as I loved Elizabeth. She was so much fun, easy going, and so engaging wherever she was I asked myself, "Could another child be as special?"

When my son, Glenn, was born, all my uncertainty evaporated. He was beautiful and I immediately felt the magic of motherhood re-appear. (Do I sound like I was a proud mother?) At two days old, however, Glenn showed signs of jaundice. My first pediatrician told me to stop nursing immediately. He went on to say that if I didn't listen my son would be at risk. Not believing that for a minute, I changed doctors. Within two weeks Glenn's condition improved considerably and the daily blood tests that had been required ceased.

Glenn was quite active throughout his youth. He certainly had his fair share of bruises, stitches, and scars. At the time, his dad and I thought all of these experiences were perfectly normal for a boy and didn't really give it that much attention. These occurrences plus a collapsed lung at age 16, however, were early signs of a disorder that would later be diagnosed.

I didn't nurse Elizabeth so I was pleased when Glenn and I shared the special bond nursing fosters. I would hold him for hours during the night and marvel at his beauty and specialness. He was nursed for almost his entire first year. I stopped when he started to bite. Boy, did that hurt!

As Glenn got older, we saw no indication of jealousy between him and Elizabeth. He had beautiful large eyes, light brown hair, and developed the same outgoing personality his sister had. She took care of him as his big sister. I have lots of pictures of her arms around her brother, Glenn.

Having It All

While child rearing for us at such a young age was trial and error, I believe we did a great job. We enjoyed our children, shared responsibilities, traveled back and forth to our Connecticut family, and had lots of friends. As time went on, however, I did miss teaching, having left the profession after working for less than a year when I became pregnant with Elizabeth.

Glenn was two years old and Elizabeth was starting kindergarten when I returned to the classroom. I engaged a neighborhood grandmother to watch Glenn during the day and Elizabeth after her morning session. It's hard to believe today, but I had no qualms about allowing Elizabeth to walk the three blocks to her babysitter when she got out of school. Safety was not an issue nor a concern at that time.

Glenn had other children with whom to play in the morning and by the time his sister arrived, he was usually already up from his nap and jumping up and down to see her. (They were always connected!) We had created an easy schedule, a safe, loving environment, and I was able to balance work and motherhood reasonably well. All the pieces of my life, including the schools (mine and Elizabeth's) were close by. I saw myself as capable, competent, happy, fortunate, and having it all.

We eventually moved to a larger home in a more upscale environment in suburban Maryland. Elizabeth was in 2nd grade and Glenn was ready for pre-school. My husband, Irv was building his CPA practice and I was teaching 6th grade. We then hired a woman to be a live-in nanny.

We were a true, young 1970s family, our time filled with school and after-school activities. It was a busy life, but we managed. My husband pitched in a lot and I felt great about being both a mother and an educator. In 1979, when Glenn was 9 and Elizabeth 12, I earned my master's degree. I treasured my family and I treasured my husband. All of this wouldn't have been possible if he hadn't willingly taken over many responsibilities so I could handle the additional workload.

Life Gives Us A Shock

From the outside everything seemed wonderful. Signs of our marriage drifting didn't occur until much later. My husband's CPA practice became quite successful. His work, however, required an increase in the amount of time away from home. On one side, his work responsibilities and clients were pulling at him, while on the other, I became more demanding of his time. All in all, it seemed like we were leading two different lives. I felt abandoned and he felt unappreciated.

We began married life and parenting at such a young age. Here we were 20+ years later, feeling overloaded and distanced from each other. Perhaps we could have worked it out, but then my husband's older (and only) brother died at age 47. He had a very difficult time recovering emotionally after that.

Irv began to question his life and the responsibilities he felt saddled with. He felt he had started so young building a business that he missed the good things in life along the way. Elizabeth was already in college and Glenn was a high school senior. We could see, shortly down the road, it would just be "us." We made an effort at couple counseling, but he was already on his way out of the marriage. It was a very difficult time for all of us, including him.

He asked me for a divorce. I can still picture Irv walking up the stairs from our finished basement looking back at me seated on the coach. He was telling me to take care and that he'd be in touch. It was all so civilized. We never engaged an attorney. We used the services of a mediator. We carved out an agreement in three sessions. To this day, we remain good friends.

I had no idea how to face life without my husband. All my adult time I was part of a couple. All the decisions and arrangements in my life were made as a couple. Irv took care of me and now I had to take care of myself. I really didn't know how. I was the coordinator in our family, but he was the glue. I had relied so heavily on his judgment, his financial capability, and his emotional support that I didn't even have my own checkbook. While my struggle seemed without end, Glenn was still home completing his senior year in high school. He was orchestrating his college plans, being as supportive as possible under difficult circumstances and trying to finish what should have been a very exciting time. He experienced my pain along with his own. Talk about connection.

Over the years, we have stuck together as a family. I love connecting with my children. To this day, Glenn and Elizabeth feel close, their love for each other is evident. In their relationship, one can easily see the power of connection.

The Dance of Interdependence

It's a complicated dance step we're learning as we combine family, our separate lives, work, relationships, and understanding ourselves. Sometimes it seems as if I'm trying to do the tango, the mambo, the waltz, the jitterbug, and ballet, with the macarena thrown in for good measure. The challenge comes in incorporating and honoring the multi-faceted patterns of relating to all the people in my life.

Much of how well we dance these steps has to do with how well we dance the *dance of interdependence* in our first, most significant system — our family.

A year after Glenn moved from Pennsylvania where he had been working, to Chicago, he suffered a serious bicycle accident. This resulted in a separated shoulder and internal bleeding on his injured hip. Glenn saw several doctors during his hospital stay. Thankfully, an astute pediatrician/genecist recognized the unusualness of his condition. After a thorough history he clinically diagnosed Glenn with Ehlers-Danlos Syndrome Type IV. Additional tests including a tissue analysis confirmed his diagnosis. Ehlers-Danlos Syndrome (EDS) is an extremely rare disorder that occurs in fewer than one in 20,000 people. EDS has multiple categories. Those with Type IV are born without the ability to manufacture the necessary amount of collagen for normal connective tissue development in the body. They are born with connective tissue that is inherently more fragile and susceptible to injury. Because the body's circulatory, digestive, and uterine systems are comprised of connective tissue, EDS Type IV can be life threatening.

With no indicators of family members having Ehlers-Danlos Syndrome, the doctor told Glenn his condition resulted from a "spontaneous mutation". In other words, he didn't inherit the disease. He is, however, now a carrier.

As Glenn's mom I wanted to immediately take care of him. I brought books to his attention. I asked him to consider alternative medical practices. I even invited him to join me on a spiritual/healing weekend. While Glenn wanted my support, at the same time he was determined to take care of himself. We were engrossed in our dance of trying to find out which steps were needed for interdependence and which were the steps needed for independence.

What a dance! How does one begin to assess the delicate balance between assisting and encouraging self-sufficiency? Where does "helping" become "hindering"? How does one differentiate between "caring" and "interfering"?

I sought help. I found out through counseling with my good friend, Dr. Jill, that in figuring out my role and my relationship with Glenn, I was also finding answers for my own healing! I had to learn that, instead of taking so much responsibility for my son, I needed to be taking responsibility for myself. I needed to learn new ways to be supportive in a non-judgmental way.

In time, I was able to release control over Glenn's destiny to Glenn where it belonged. I began to acknowledge a power greater than either of us for what we, together, were learning and facing. We began trusting each other. I developed belief that Glenn would do what he needed to do, make the right choices, and know what was best for him. I also restored my faith in God that my son was in his care and that no matter what, Glenn would be all right.

The Family Comes Together

As mentioned earlier, Glenn, living in a small Pennsylvania town, had worked for over four years with a company that marketed athletic training equipment. In 1997, a year before his bicycle accident, Glenn was ready to make some career changes. With the encouragement of his sister and brother-in-law, Ron, Glenn decided to take a few days off and visit them in Chicago for a long weekend. He immediately fell in love with the city. He became excited about the possibilities Chicago could offer him and about living near family. He saw the move as a wonderful opportunity on multiple levels. Within a matter of weeks, Glenn left his job, terminated his lease and moved to the Windy City. Knowing that Glenn was living close to Elizabeth and Ron was, in and of itself, a huge blessing in my life. They loved the Chicago area and felt quite settled in their suburban community. At the time Ron was working for a large law firm and Elizabeth was working with a non-profit, Chicago Cares. Glenn became the director of a business center designed to employ physically challenged adults. Three years later Elizabeth took maternity leave to care for her son, Eli, born in March of 2000.

Moving On

Shortly after becoming a new dad, Ron accepted a position with an emerging dot-com company. In spite of what appeared to be a great opportunity, the company eventually closed and Ron and Elizabeth faced new career choices. They decided he'd look for a position with a law firm in Atlanta where Phil and I had moved in the summer of 1995. In addition to us, Ron's brother, his wife, and nephew were also living in Atlanta. When we received the phone call with the surprising news they were "looking to consider a change" we were overjoyed. I never imagined my daughter and her family would consider living close by and that we could connect regularly.

They had made several trips to Atlanta while Ron interviewed with various firms. This gave Elizabeth and I time to be together. On one particular hot, summer day, Elizabeth asked me to go for a long walk with her and Eli. It would provide us time to have a conversation without any interruption.

We walked and talked for over two hours. We walked along a nearby lake and talked and talked and talked. It was important for Elizabeth to feel assured that her living nearby wouldn't jeopardize our relationship or create unfair expectations. Then she asked me a question that caught me off guard. She wanted *my* opinion on what *I thought* my role as her mom should be!

I took a few minutes to consider my answer. Then it came to me. What was important for me to say, and for Elizabeth to hear, was not what I thought my role as mom should be, but rather, to ask what she needed from me. I wanted her to take the lead. After all, it was her life and she would know best how she'd like to see my role. Sharing her thoughts, hopes, and ideas would give me the option of choosing what I'd be willing to do to support her.

Some of her answers included discussing private issues, eliminating unfair expectations, and being close while maintaining her independence. We assured each other that all of us being together was cause for celebration. We didn't want miscommunication to ruin our relationship. We hugged, got excited over the pleasures that would result from living in the same city, and agreed to always trust each other with the truth, no matter what. She told me their plan was to relocate as soon as Ron landed the right position. Only a few months later, the Ron and Elizabeth Lieberman family moved to Atlanta.

What a wonderful homecoming! I felt so blessed to have her near. I was so happy! We had been given an opportunity to reconnect in our own way — the best we knew how to do, sticking our toes in the water, overcoming past patterns of miscommunication, and having a second chance. Once they settled in, Elizabeth resumed her position as Conference Director with Net Impact, a nonprofit organization.

Not long afterwards, Glenn also moved from Chicago to join us in Atlanta. Today we all share special occasions and holidays. My second husband Phil and I continue to play an important role in helping raise Eli and his baby brother Isaac. We continue to support each other by honoring our individuality, our space, and our lives.

The Balancing Act

Feeling connected is powerful, especially today when people feel so isolated.

How many people do you know who have been separated by physical location or emotional distance? How many are estranged from relatives or loved ones and may be yearning to get together? Sometimes it seems we have to disconnect in order to be motivated to reconnect in more satisfactory or intimate ways.

As we participate in life's journey, we're planning, learning, or reviewing. We can't stand still in that process. We can't know where to make advancements if we don't take time to look at where we've been and where we are now. Learning precedes change. Acknowledging and accepting change creates new behavior.

Still, it's exciting to realize we create our future based on the lessons of our past and expand our reality based on the lessons of today.

Pay Attention to Family

Obviously, our lives aren't neatly segmented into convenient linear compartments. Wouldn't it be nice if we could live in a series of projects and accomplishments simultaneously?

"Let's see. First, we'll take care of healing our past family relationships. Oh, good, that's done. Now let's move on to healing the globe!"

It just doesn't work that way!

Life is an organic, flowing process of interrelating and healing while it happens. It flows while we interact with our families and while we contribute service to our communities. Achieving that balance of personal, family, work, and community life challenges all of us. How do we discern who we are as individuals, differentiate ourselves from our spouses, family units and social groups, and still contribute and benefit from the whole? It's a precarious tightrope act.

Each of us has "issues". We all engage in different parts of our lives at different times. Sometimes our focus is on work, sometimes on family and sometimes on our causes and contributions. The dilemma comes when one interest or another insists on our attention or we find ourselves unintentionally neglecting important people in order to put our focus on other things.

This has been an issue and testing ground for me and my children because I have been so enthusiastically involved in a multitude of projects. Elizabeth and Glenn have told me at times they feel excluded because of my choices. They have also been forthcoming in their pride. I'm continuously balancing my involvements with my priorities.

I was especially thrilled the final day of my 3Day Walk when Elizabeth, Ron and Eli cheered me as I got close to the finish line. It was an experience I'll never forget. That special moment was months in preparation. The experience changed my life. My children knew how hard I had worked and how much it meant to me to complete my commitment. They honored me and were with me to applaud my success.

As my life evolves and I'm faced with new considerations, I have to remind myself that every choice I make has a ripple effect. This is a reality we all face every day

I've learned that when we move ahead, our spirits

and bodies move ahead with us. Yet our lives are made up of more than ourselves. Others in our lives may not be moving at the same speed or on the same road. I found this in my relationship with my adult children.

Talk with any parent whose teenagers are close to leaving home and you will find a mixture of excitement and sadness. We look forward to the freedom that will come when they live their lives out of our hearth. Yet we shudder at the thought they won't be a daily part of our lives.

Even though my children are "grown," I wonder if parenting is ever over. Maybe there's truth to the saying, "When kids are young the challenges are small; the older they get, the bigger the challenges." I'm grateful I didn't hear that message until *after* my children were born! I hope that as you read this, regardless of whether you're someone's child or someone's parent, you'll recognize you're not alone in facing this dilemma.

Advising Grown Children

It's a universal truth. We all want the best for our families. Our children want their parents to be healthy, happy, and self-sufficient. As parents, we want our children to experience the same well-being. I want to be sure that in expressing my concerns to my children, they know my intention is one of *caring* and not one of *interfering*. Of course nagging questions remain. Is there an appropriate way to offer advice when it's unsolicited? How does one create and build the trust that allows communication to remain open and respected — not shut down and rejected?

After all these years, my mom, Lillian, is still my best friend. I can ask her for advice and she will give me her best shot. When she offers me her unsolicited point of view, I listen. While we may not always be in agreement, we respect each other and maintain open communication.

On the other hand, as a parent, I view things from a completely different perspective. I realize that adult children need to be independent and make their own decisions, but certain questions come with that realization. When they ask for your advice, do they really want it, or are they just looking to see if you agree with what they've already decided? Whatever the answer, they want our approval regardless of what we really think!

I've decided that, before I give my children solicited or unsolicited advice, I'm going to first reassure them that my opinion comes from a place of caring not interfering, and then ask for their permission before giving my true feelings. After that, the choices they make are up to them.

SECTION 4

Entrepreneurial Connections

Becoming an Entrepreneur

Sometimes, the building of our legacies is a matter of doing the work we choose step by step, doing it well, and raising the bar. Why be average when you are capable of being excellent? For me, excellence is not about perfection. It's about doing my personal best in every endeavor, then experiencing fulfillment.

All of us have experienced "defining moments" in our lives. Mine came in the spring of 1976 while I was still teaching.

At the request of my daughter, Elizabeth, I took a personal day to attend her school field trip. While I don't recall where we actually went, I vividly remember sitting next to Elizabeth's teacher during the one-hour bus trip. Both of us shared stories about our situations and what we saw as our future in teaching.

She went on to tell me that she was enrolled in an innovative master's degree program being offered by a college in Scranton, Pennsylvania. It was being "piloted" in the Washington, D.C. area specifically for teachers. Classes were held on weekends and during the summer months as part of a three-year program. The professors were actually located in D.C. and employed by Merrywood College. My daughter's teacher was completing her first year and loving it. I immediately became interested in getting all the information and pursuing the degree for myself.

The decision to earn my master's degree through this program was a major one. With a full-time teaching position, two children (ages nine and six), a household to manage, and a marriage to protect, I had my doubts. The plan would require significant family support. My husband was totally willing to do his part so I decided to go for it.

With a commitment of three weekends a month — every month, year round — the program was almost full time. I stuck with it and, after writing my thesis, graduated in June, 1979. I was so proud of my accomplishment! I knew I'd done my personal best. From that experience, I learned that excellence is achieved through self-motivation and habit. This experience also proved something I think I always knew: *Excellence is within your reach when you simply do your best.*

Remember, everything you do is a personal statement of your talent, belief, and dedication. Your name is attached to every task you undertake. If you raise your standards, you'll deliver more than you had ever thought possible.

Time for a Career Change

In 1983, four years after earning my master's degree, I left teaching to begin my journey as an entrepreneur. While it wasn't a quick decision, there were unexpected circumstances that led up to my making a career change. Had you asked me during my years in the classroom if I'd ever thought about doing something else, I would have said "no." It just goes to show that change has a way of creeping up on us and presents choices when we least expect them. This is what happened.

In early April, 1983, I woke up on a school day in excruciating lower abdominal pain. I probably should have told my husband but it was tax season and I didn't want to overload him with more stress beyond what he already had. (If you think that sounds strange, you've never been married to a CPA.)

I called my school and told them I had to take a sick day. The only regular physician I had was my gynecologist/obstetrician so I placed a call to his administrator and begged for an appointment. Sensing my pain, she told me to come in right away.

Sheer determination got me to his office through the relentless pain I felt. While I knew I wasn't pregnant, it was obvious that something was very, very wrong. After a thorough internal exam, my doctor told me to get dressed and meet him in his office.

The Unexpected

He started out by acknowledging how much pain I was in and asked why my husband had not driven me. I reminded him it was tax season and that I thought I could handle this on my own. Then I got the news I had barely expected. My doctor said I'd developed a large tumor on my only ovary (The other ovary had been removed years before because of a similar growth; I was certain lightning couldn't strike twice). He suggested I have a hysterectomy as soon as possible but also encouraged me to get another opinion. He gave me the name and number of a doctor with a practice close by and had his administrator make the call for me and arrange an appointment at his request. A second exam confirmed the first diagnosis.

I was 39 years old. I was frightened. I felt alone and vulnerable. I was given medication to relieve the pain and sent on my way to inform my husband of the morning's events and to make a decision — as if I had a choice!

Driving to my husband's office was very difficult. I was a mess. I had cried from home to the doctor and from the doctor to his office. When I walked in, the receptionist took one look at me and asked, "Bonnie, what's wrong?"

"I've got to talk to my husband right away."

I walked down the hall into his office, closed the door, and sobbed uncontrollably. Of course, he had no idea what my emotional outburst was all about. Once I told him what was going on, I started to apologize.

"I know it's tax season. I know you're busy. I know the timing sucks. But I can't wait 10 days (until the end of tax season)," I said.

To his credit, he did his best to ease my comfort. It was easy for me to sense, however, that I had "picked" an inconvenient time to have surgery. I don't recall his asking me why I went to the doctor alone, or his being upset that I didn't ask him to be with me. But it was clear that having surgery before the end of tax season would be a major encumbrance during an already stressful time.

My mother saved the day. She arrived the day after the surgery and helped me tremendously during my first week home. Elizabeth was almost 16 and Glenn was 13, so much of her support was in allowing me time to rest and regain my strength.

The principal of the school where I worked treated me wonderfully throughout the ordeal. I had earned over six weeks of sick leave and many days of personal leave time. With all of those days in my account, he encouraged me to take the rest of the school year off. What a blessing!

My Future Arrived in a Classified Ad: Mail Boxes, Etc.

Once I felt better, I provided lesson plans for an extended-stay substitute teacher and began to think about my life, career, and future (It's amazing how clear your mind can get when you spend time away from your usual environment). I began to realize that teaching had become more challenging over time. I'd lost the spark of excitement I once had. I'd become restless to do something else.

Both Irv I had grown up in families where our parents owned their own businesses. Once in a while, we'd talk about how "some day" I might have a business of my own.

One evening, Irv clipped a small ad from the newspaper and shared it with me. It was a "business opportunity" ad, promoting "a new, revolutionary franchise." The ad said that a San Diego-based company was looking to expand into the D.C. area. The franchise name was *Mail Boxes, Etc.*

At that time things were still good in our marriage. In fact, my husband showed tremendous support in my changing careers and was quick to encourage me. While the last thing I ever expected was to finish the last two months of school on sick leave, I later realized it was just a matter of time before I would have moved on anyway. Rather than quit, I got approval to take a year's leave of absence. While this meant receiving no pay, it did ensure I'd have a teaching position at the end of that period if I chose to activate my contract. Therefore, I had until the following spring (1984) to decide what I wanted to do.

I never went back. I never looked back!

Mail Boxes, Etc. has become well known and renamed The UPS Store. But it was unknown in the early '80s. I was curious about it and responded to the ad the next day. The recruiter talked about the opportunities for growth with Mail Boxes, Etc., and told me about the possibility of having territorial rights and income from multiple locations. With my husband's backing, I decided to open my first franchise. The first store became so successful I quickly I opened my second store 10 months later.

By purchasing the "territorial or area rights," I not only had the option of developing more stores for myself, but also the right to sell the franchise to other perspective buyers. After 12 years, I had 28 stores to my credit, owning six of my own at various times.

Like any business, I dealt with lots of challenges. However, I absolutely loved the connections I made. I would connect customers with one another, promote their businesses to each other, and get to know the regulars who frequented our stores. Customers became family. Talk about making connections!

Freedom of Being My Own Boss

When my year's leave of absence from teaching was up and I got a call inviting me to return to the classroom, I was already on an entrepreneurial roll and had no intention of giving that up. While teaching offered non-working snow days, long weekends, holidays, and summer vacations, being my own boss provided *freedom*. Besides, I loved being connected with the business community.

In the early 1980s, I had taken a huge risk, stepped out in faith, and become a pioneer. I demonstrated respect and appreciation for my employees and customers. Being an active connector in my stores and in the community was not only a wonderful experience but it offered me significant financial and personal rewards.

All was not sunshine and roses, though. It was during the late 80's my marriage broke up and I had to deal with all the related issues. By the time the summer of '95 arrived, I had remarried, sold my entire operation back to the corporate office of Mail Boxes, Etc., and moved to Atlanta.

Mail Boxes, Etc. was my first entrepreneurial endeavor. It set the stage for other innovative endeavors and told me I wouldn't go back to conventional income-producing activities. I followed this franchising experience with network marketing. Those two industries shaped and reinforced my belief that, to really be successful, you have to develop the ability to *connect*. Every worthwhile relationship is built on the strength of the people willing to connect with one another. I strongly believe the key to one's success in life directly relates to the degree one can *connect with others effectively!*

Urgency in Business

In the business world, especially among women, there's an urgent need and desire to forsake the old paradigm of cutthroat competition. We're getting fed up with fighting others, protecting ourselves, and living in the fear that there isn't enough to go around — not enough for me.

In the August 2002 issue of *Fast Company* magazine, Margaret Heffernan gives us these remarkable statistics and facts about men and women in the corporate world:

- The wage gap between male and female managers actually widened in the prosperous years between 1995 and 2000.
- Only 4% of the top earners at Fortune 500 companies are women.
- Women fill only 7.3% of the total line positions held by corporate officers. Between 1992 and 2000, the number of sexual harassment claims increased by 50%.
- By 2005, the article said, there will be about 4.7 million self-employed women in the United States, up 77% since 1983. The increase for men? Just 6%.

Heffernan notes that "women leave their companies and their positions because they want to work differently... Women don't want to redecorate the company. They want to build something new, different, and theirs — from scratch."

Women Still Try to Play Like Men

One powerful entrepreneur who runs her own fashion company told me, "Historically, women have supported each other through friends and family and charities and socials, but when they get into the work arena, they change. They revert to the good ol' boys rules, where they figure anything goes in order to win. They'll forsake their visions of their loftier ideals and dreams for themselves and turn on each other, often becoming very manipulative."

Still, this businesswoman refuses to let the situation among her female colleagues get her down. She tries to keep her attitude "up" and works to create an environment where positive attitudes reign.

She continues, "Many of my friends and I have been working so hard to get rid of negativity, but so many still haven't. It's getting to the point where I refuse to have such gloom and doom around me. I work with people and encourage them to adopt a more positive attitude. If they don't, I suggest they would be happy elsewhere."

That businesswoman is forward thinking. I am also working to change the old patterns. Other women are joining me and we are doing something about it. Women are coming together in what I call "The Joy of Connecting" groups to help each other build their dreams. They're fostering their inherent supportive natures and taking nurturing to a new level — to care for themselves, yes, but also to grow out of their fears and help other women in the workplace. Doing this means making the powerful choice to take charge of life's journeys and connect in truthful, non-manipulative, ways.

From the Back Fence to the Front Yard

Marina Hodgini is an energy coach and speaker; a petite dynamite package. I find it amazing how quickly she can read a person's energy level. Her work is about expanding those energy levels, which increases productivity. (I find it fascinating that somebody actually knows how to do that!)

She's a quintessential entrepreneur who refuses to see obstacles, but rather sees possibilities. She keeps asking, "How can we solve this?" She has always searched for solutions in her own life and in others'. Even at the age of 18, she was into personal growth. She knew she wanted to do more than what everybody was telling her she should be doing.

"My father thought I'd be a great nurse because my uncle owned a hospital in Chicago. He said that would be a terrific way for me to meet a husband. And that really didn't even begin to fit who I was, but it was a real neat package for him. So, when somebody has written a script for you and you really don't think it's your play, you've got to reach out to some other sources to get some new material. I sought support and solutions in therapy at 18. I found out: Don't wait for the boat to come to you — go out and swim to the boat!"

I doubt that most women ever have the benefit of a conversation like this, which is another reason for "The Joy of Connecting" gatherings. When I thought of starting these get-togethers during which women could share their hopes, dreams, desires, challenges, and anything else, this was exactly the kind of conversation I thought would happen.

Marina agrees that women need these conversations. She said, "Women have always connected over the back fence, but now we're connecting with intention and with a purpose that we're defining. Our intention before was for support on a personal, home basis, but I think given our involvement in the business arena, we've taken it to a broader level. This broader level is in multiple tiers that says we can also support each other in business — in our passions and dreams and careers and in our finances."

When women think of connecting in business, it's not just for making more money (though that would be nice). We see the business world as a place where people (not just women) can grow as human beings. The environment encourages them to work together to create more for everybody.

In her *Fast Company* article, Heffernan, who has run five businesses in the U.S. and the U.K., sums up what this type of environment could mean for all of us.

"If (the current) way of doing business is indeed broken . . . then we had all better hope that this parallel universe is almost complete. We may need it sooner than we thought we would. And it sure looks like a lot more fun."

Women Communicate Differently

When my husband Phil and I travel by air, we both like to have aisle seats. Whenever possible we request aisles across from one another.

It's a perfect arrangement. We each have flexibility to move around and more leg space. It's fun to compare notes on who had the most interesting side passenger. On one particularly long flight, it was obvious that Phil was really enjoying talking with the man next to him. Every time I looked over, they were engaged in conversation.

About two hours into the flight, I got up to use the restroom. I leaned over to kiss Phil and asked to be introduced to his "new friend." To my dismay, Phil had no idea what the gentleman's name was. They had spoken continuously for half the flight and never introduced themselves to each other!

Our ways of "connecting" are as different as our genders. I can't imagine two women sitting next to each other and not exchanging names! In two hours we'd likely know each other's life stories.

It's a known fact that men and women communicate differently. Several books have been written about it, with one noting that sometimes the two genders speak as if they're from different planets. We differ in the way we do business, the way we give and get advice, and the way we network.

Women are connectors by nature. We exchange ideas, recipes, leads, resources, experiences, and anything else we can to support each other. We can learn more from each other in a bathroom visit than men learn spending an entire day playing golf together.

Entrepreneurs are connectors. They recognize and value the power of networking. They build relationships with ease. Because entrepreneurs know first hand the challenge of being on one's own, I believe they collectively recognize how much they rely on one another.

Consciously doing business with women fosters its own connection. Spending money to support a woman-owned business or enterprise is one way to ensure her success. We often get to know more about a woman when we purchase her service or product. The reason is because connecting is about much more than a purchase; it's a woman's way of being with another.

Unlike men, women like to know the *whole* story!

SECTION 5

A Lifetime Love Connection

The Beginning of a Lifetime Love Affair

It was a Sunday evening in late January 1989. I had been visiting my parents in Florida for the weekend, and had returned to my home in suburban Maryland earlier in the day.

Being the Mail Boxes, Etc. entrepreneur that I was, I decided to go to the store to catch up on paperwork. I told the young female student living with me that if anyone called, ask that person to reach me at my store. I had just started going through my mail and messages when the phone rang. I picked it up expecting it was a local friend welcoming me home. What I didn't expect was this phone call would change my life forever.

The voice I heard at the other end was a surprise. I recognized it despite not having heard it for years.

"Hi Bonnie . . ."

"Is this Phil Parker?" I asked.

"Yes," was his reply.

Making My Ultimate Connection

Phil and I had known each other years earlier when we were married to other spouses and raising our families in the same community in suburban Maryland. Both being young marrieds with children, we used to participate together in family activities and maintained a social life among our peer group.

The Parkers ended up moving to Atlanta in the mid-1970s and we lost touch. Years passed and, in January 1989, Phil returned single to the D.C. area. He had stayed in touch with some wonderful mutual friends, Mollie and Dennis, and contacted them. He became divorced in 1984 and had spent five years in Germany working on a project for a Virginia-based company. With the project completed, he was back in the States reporting to the home office.

Mollie immediately invited him for a Friday night dinner. As one would expect, the talk moved to "old times" and the "what and where" of all his past friends — "What's so and so doing now? How are so and so?"

Eventually, he asked, "How are Bonnie and Irv?" They innocently related the news. "Oh, you don't know? Bonnie is now divorced and has started her own business." Of course, Phil had no idea, having been away for more than 15 years. Recalling me and my "young body" (ha ha ha), he asked for my phone number and called me that same weekend.

Fate Answers the Phone

"I can't believe you're calling me. How did you get this number? Where are you?" I asked, astonished.

"I'm in D.C., and got your home number from Mollie and Dennis," he answered calmly. "When I called you earlier, your roommate said it was fine to reach you at your office and gave me this number."

I began asking questions in rapid succession. "What are you doing here? Why are you calling after such a long time? Are you still living in Atlanta? *Are you married?*"

"Slow down!" he said. "I'm single and I heard you are as well. I'd like to see you."

I thought, why not? "What do you have in mind?" I asked. We agreed to meet for dinner two days later. He agreed to pick me up after work.

I hung up the phone, stunned. Fifteen years had passed. So much time and so much change. I could barely remember what Phil looked like except that he had dark hair and was short. I thought about how much fun it would be to reconnect with an old friend and catch up. I smiled with anticipation.

It was mid-morning the following day when the phone rang.

"Good morning, Mail Boxes Etc., how can I help you?"

"Hi Bonnie, it's Phil."

"Oh, hi," I replied, not sure why he was calling.

"Listen, I was thinking, why wait until tomorrow night to get together? How about lunch today?"

Not having any lunch plans of my own, I said, "Is that in lieu of or in addition to Tuesday's dinner?"

"Both" was Phil's reply.

"How do you know you'll want to take me out twice?"

Without missing a beat he said, "I'll take my chances." We agreed to meet at one o'clock.

Love Over Lunch

I had no reason to believe that our lunch would be anything more than two old friends getting together (two now-*single* friends, yes, but two old friends just the same). But when Phil walked into my store that afternoon, I felt excited to see him. I didn't remember him being so handsome and his warm hug and kiss on the cheek felt wonderful. Wow! Phil Parker taking me to lunch after all this time!

We walked up the street to a soup/sandwich shop and for more than two hours talked about everything — our divorces, our children, our careers, and so much more. We immediately re-established the relationship we had shared years before. It was comfortable and inviting. If it had not been a workday, we probably would have spent several more hours together.

Phil walked me back to the store, thanked me for a wonderful lunch, and told me he'd call later that evening. For the rest of the day, I anticipated continuing our conversation. We talked again later that night and both of us eagerly looked forward to our dinner date the following evening. I carefully picked out my next day's outfit and went to bed excited.

I had selected dining at a Chinese restaurant. Phil came by just as I was getting ready to close the store. He helped me with a few odds and ends and we were off. While I don't remember the details of that dinner or the conversation, I do know I felt very alive and comfortable being with Phil. I was already anticipating becoming closer.

That night, we were the last couple to leave the restaurant. Phil drove me to my car, we exchanged a passionate kiss, said goodnight, and promised to talk the following day.

Within a matter of weeks my life had changed. Phil was becoming part of my routine, as eager to see me as I was to be with him. We laughed, talked, hugged, and kissed. My days were filled with work; my evenings filled with Phil. Within three weeks, Phil and I wanted and needed to be together and he moved into my home. My roommate, Caroline, had her own apartment in the lower level of the house!

The Connection Disconnects

We both worked during the day. Evenings were ours. Every day was special. I found myself falling in love all over again. Then the unthinkable happened.

Phil decided our relationship was going too fast. He got scared. He became unsure and announced he'd accepted a position with a large corporation and was moving to Atlanta.

I couldn't believe it. I felt hurt and angry. Just when I'd begun to feel relaxed and trusting, Phil was leaving. Our six weeks together ended with both of us in tears. With his car packed, Phil left.

I felt embarrassed, abandoned, and used. Was our love affair over? Phil had shown me that I could love again. But could I ever *trust* again?

I returned to my old routine. Soon after Phil settled into his new job, he started to call. Every day he'd call to check in to make certain I was okay and to fill me in on his new activities. In the meantime, I had decided to participate in the singles scene, which was designed to make Phil jealous. Actually, it proved to be disastrous.

I couldn't get Phil out of my mind. Each evening, I eagerly anticipated hearing his voice. Since his new job included travel to the D.C. area, he was able to visit me often. While we wanted to be together, Phil wanted his freedom, too. This scenario lasted 18 months, consisting of daily calls, monthly visits, passionate lovemaking, and separation.

Then one day, life changed again. In November, 1991, just before my birthday, Phil called. He begged me to visit him the upcoming weekend. I agreed to make the trip. When I arrived, he told me for the first time that he loved me and that he wanted to spend the rest of his life with me. Would I welcome him back if he were to get a new job in D.C.?

I was so excited, I could hardly breathe. *Phil loves me. Phil wants to be with me.* Of course, I said, "Yes. I want to be with you, too. I hate having a long distance relationship." So with some careful planning, I returned later that month to Atlanta, helped him pack his things, and we drove back to D.C. together.

It took about two weeks before the moving truck with Phil's belongings arrived at our home. I was at work, and he and the workmen got everything inside. It was wonderful to come home that evening and witness Phil settling in with his books, furniture, clothing, etc. After work the next day, I pulled up to the driveway to find the front deck covered with empty boxes.

"Where shall I store all my boxes?" Phil asked as I came into the kitchen.

"What do you mean, store them?" I answered.

"Well, you know, just in case I need them" was his reply.

Without missing a beat, I replied, "You're here to stay. So throw them all out!" That was 14 years ago. We look back at that time and laugh.

A Life Together

We began what felt like married life, although it was six years later before we made it "official." Phil was offered a lucrative CEO position in — of all places — Atlanta. Both of us were ready for a change of place, work, and lifestyle. It was at that moment that we decided to marry. We would sell my business, the home we were sharing, and create a new life together.

Within a short time, we had a beautiful wedding/

brunch reception, experienced a quick honeymoon, packed up everything (I wish we had saved those packing boxes), and headed south as newlyweds. Phil began his new job and I spent the days exploring, learning my way around, and looking for places to network. After living in the same community for 30 years, this was a significant and welcomed change.

Phil had been hired to turn a company around, and things at his job progressed nicely. He made several changes that put the company on a new track. His position had benefits, and we were feeling emotionally — and financially — terrific. Suddenly, we faced a huge setback.

A New Journey for Phil

After eight months of employment, hard work, strategic planning, travel, and newly implemented systems, Phil had a meeting with his employer's Washington attorney. The attorney had been sent to Atlanta to inform him that the company had been sold and Phil's services "were no longer required." He was given a short period of time to "pack up and leave the premises." In an instant, Phil lost his position, his self-esteem, his pride, and his income. He was 56.

During this tough time, I mustered all the support I could to encourage Phil, believe in him, and keep his attitude positive. Months passed and he was unable to find a job. The employment situation in Atlanta was especially tough during this 1996 period, as the Olympics were coming to Atlanta and no one was hiring.

After his self-imposed pity party, Phil was finally willing to discuss what he might be able to do.

It was time. I was over the top with frustration

because nothing was working. We weren't communicating. Prospects were nonexistent. One evening I popped the question, "Phil, if you could do anything you want, what would it be?"

He immediately said, "I'd like to be a motivational speaker."

Just like that! Over the years, Phil had shared mesmerizing stories of experiences in school, college, the military, and his years overseas. It always amazed me listening to his vignettes how graphically Phil could tell a story. Now, out of the blue, he declared that he wanted to be a professional speaker.

Well, after catching my breath, I assured him if that was what he *really* wanted, I would support his decision. He talked about taking classes, developing techniques, learning about marketing, etc. In one afternoon, Phil went from indecision to action and I could feel his energy and excitement. He affirmed that he was prepared to do whatever it took to develop his craft. He was ready. I was ready. We had the financial resources to get started. He began making plans to begin the process.

Months passed and Phil became immersed in classes, reading, and connecting. One day, I approached Phil with another idea.

"Would you consider writing a book?" I asked.

"Are you crazy?" he replied. But the more he thought about becoming an author, the more sense it made. Speaking and also having a book to sell would be that much more effective. Another endeavor began and, after almost two years, Phil's book was published. Not only was he being paid to speak, but through his book, *Kiss Yourself Hello! A Journey From The Life of Business to The Business of Life*, his message could reach a broader audience. The next two years had its highs and lows. Through it all, I kept my faith in Phil and he maintained his belief in himself. Taking an uncharted journey together, we weathered the changing conditions, became stronger as a couple, celebrated our individuality, and created a bright future.

Phil and I have a strong connection with each other. It's consistent, enduring, and endearing. Together, we know our total commitment is stronger than the sum of the individual commitments we make. Where we are today is a result of our unwavering faith in each other. He knew he could count on me and I knew he would honor his commitments.

Were it not for the connection as neighbors early on and the connection with our mutual friends Mollie and Dennis, this partnership would never have happened. The power of our connections led to the power of our joy-filled relationship.

Ours is truly a lifetime love affair. Our commitment to each other continues to strengthen. Every day, we appreciate life and each other more. It's a connection that will last a long, long time.

Marriage: A Beautiful Union

"What greater thing is there for two human souls than to feel that they are joined for life, to strengthen each other in all labor, to rest on each other in all sorrow, to minister to each other in all pain, to be one with each other in silent unspeakable memories at the last moment of last parting?"

— George Eliot

Marriage has the power to create a beautiful union of two individuals so that they become as one. What power there is in knowing that two people in a strong marriage can lead a life together that is at once combined and at the same time individual.

Through marriage, a husband and wife build history together, and through this shared voyage create a deepening love for each other. Marriage is a continuum of time where individuality evolves into oneness.

I'm not alone in knowing what I love about being married. From conversations with dozens of successfully married couples, I hear the same thing: "What I love about being married is that our relationship is constantly reinventing itself."

Our marriage changes according to the circumstances in which we find ourselves. Sometimes I am on the giving end; sometimes on the receiving. We are passing through the stages of shared marriage by first and foremost *committing* to the relationship. For example, each of us is willing to take risks in communicating our feelings to each other. A strong marriage encourages the sharing of one's separate, real self. Self-disclosure is an act of trust that creates closeness and security.

Simply put, when my husband and I verbalize our mutual dreams, concerns, and desires, our marriage becomes stronger.

Far too often, people are married but are not truly partners. They live together but not with each other. They share lives, but they do not share *a life*. They raise a family, but do not connect.

True marital *partners* are committed, not only to their relationship, but to *each other's* growth through the span of the marriage. A strong marriage needs to exist in an environment that encourages the development of both individuals. Each partner has to feel fulfilled, affirmed, and comfortable with his or her own identity. The feeling that comes from having a separate, satisfying life with a partner who also feels self-satisfaction is wonderful.

Marriage is best served when each partner grows individually while both partners grow together. It's about empathy, closeness, acceptance, flexibility, and appreciation for each other. Marriage thrives when there's trust, open communication, stability, caring, emotional security, and the realization of not being alone.

I like "belonging" exclusively to my husband while simultaneously creating my own life's purpose. It's like a kite's string securely held to the ground while the kite is able to move, explore, and experience the sky. The kite is both free and secure.

A great marriage offers the same kind of freedom and security while tethering each partner to the other. It thrives on each partner's accomplishments, supports each individual's setbacks, and fosters equality.

Like partners in a dance, great marriage partners rarely step on each other's toes, but when they do, they accept the mistake with a smile and make the best of it.

I wish for you a marriage with all that I have described. I wish for you the ability to find the common denominators in your relationship. I wish for you the stamina, strength, and faith that will allow you to do the work every great marriage requires.

In today's uncertain world, if you have the good fortune of being in a fulfilling partnership, I encourage you to treasure your partner and your relationship. It will be the finest connection you'll ever have.

My Love in Poetry

Through the years, I've discovered that one of my favorite ways to express myself is through poetry. It brings out my intimate thoughts and emotions in a way that doesn't happen when writing prose. It is a beautiful way to communicate.

This poetry relates to my feelings about my marriage and my husband Phil. I am pleased to share three poems with you.

Listening

You're reading the paper
And I say, "I need to talk to you."
You reply, "Go ahead, I'm listening."

You're working on your checkbook
And I say, "I want to tell you something."
You reply, "Go ahead, I'm listening."

You're watching television
And I say, "I have a request to make."
You reply, "Go ahead, I'm listening."

Please stop what you're doing.
Look at me.
Care for me.
Give me some time.

I need all of you
When I share all of me.
Please listen.
Not with your ears alone,
But with your heart.

Intimate Moments

I like talking
When we make love.
Sharing secrets
Expressing needs
Imaginings.

I like candlelight
When we make love
The softness
The warmth
Shadows.

I like music
When we make love
Romantic words
Quiet sounds
Movement.

Please want to know
What pleases me
When we make love.
I will tell you
Show you
Share.

I Need You

I need you
In small, little ways
Your touch
Your smile
Your kiss.

I need you
In other ways
Your tenderness
Your faith
Your understanding.

I need you in special ways
Acceptance when I'm not loving
Confidence when I'm quiet
Trust when I've disappointed you.

I need you
In all ways
To be myself
To grow and change
To be happy.

I need you
Not for what you give me
Not to exhaust you
Nor to be smothered by you.
But because I can only be me
When you are with me.

Cultivating Community Connections

Women to Women: Cultivating Our Community

It began on Mother's Day 2000. Bruce Berns, Phil, and I decided to have breakfast at The Atlanta Bread Company in Vinings, Georgia, to get caught up with what was going on in our lives. Bruce was the Publisher of *The Gazette*, a suburban bi-weekly newspaper in the Atlanta area.

It was fun for me to sit back and enjoy the camaraderie we share, listening to the two men talk about sports, politics, and Phil's speaking career. What I didn't anticipate was what followed after Bruce turned and asked about me.

Can you relate to the experience of someone inviting you to share, and then you suddenly feel your heart open up, leaving you totally vulnerable? That's what happened that Sunday morning.

The Birth of an Idea

Since my 55th birthday the previous November, I'd been struggling with questions about my life's purpose, fulfillment, and legacy. I shared with Bruce that in spite of a full schedule, lots of friends, and a steady income from my home-based business, I was still feeling unsure of the "why" of my existence. I wanted to know what I could be doing to feel greater fulfillment and contribute more. Knowing how much I love connecting and meeting people and how committed I am to women and women's issues, Bruce asked permission to make a suggestion. Of course, I was eager to listen.

Talk about the timing of showing up for a breakfast invitation! Bruce mentioned that in his interest to add value to *The Gazette*, he was evaluating new opportunities. He looked directly at me and asked if I would consider creating a new section devoted to women's issues. When I said "yes," he stunned me again by offering me the title of Associate Publisher.

Have you ever had the experience of being really excited about something, feeling empowered and ready for the challenge, then suddenly moving toward doubt with a swift reality check? Well, that's what happened to me after saying "yes" to Bruce's offer.

I began doubting my ability to handle the requirements. I couldn't see how my background as a schoolteacher, franchise owner, and network marketer would provide the necessary skills to work in the publishing arena. I knew how to do lesson plans, train and motivate employees, serve my customers, and recruit. Publishing, however, was a completely new endeavor. What happens if I can't get enough writers? What will I do if advertisers don't support the section? How will I feel if readers don't like the section or my articles?

The Other Side of Doubt

There I was, bombarding myself with "what ifs!" I had to force myself to look on the other side of doubt.

"What if" readers really liked what I had to say? "What if" advertisers wanted to target women and chose *The Gazette* to meet that need? "What if" I found writers who were eager to contribute their time and ideas? I imagined what might happen if my doubts turned to self-confidence. I started to picture myself out in the community distributing *The Gazette*, meeting prospective advertisers and sorting through submissions.

Soon my excitement overshadowed my hesitancy. What did I have to lose? How much would I gain by meeting the challenge? The timing was perfect.

I could use my previous experiences as subjects for my column. Over the years, I had done significant marketing for Mail Boxes, Etc. so soliciting ads didn't seem that overwhelming. I already knew many authors, writers, coaches, and businesswomen who would welcome the opportunity to share their ideas in print in exchange for a by-line. My excitement increased. As I told more people about the project and what I wanted, I got both encouragement and support. We gave ourselves three months to build the section and then launch it.

An Exciting Reality

The section — **"Women to Women: Cultivating Our Community"** — became a reality. We developed this mission statement: "To inspire, empower, educate women, and to support their initiatives and acknowledge their accomplishments."

The section would give women a vehicle to connect with one another! Once I put out my intention to "the universe," some of the most dynamite women I knew responded. To this day, I continue to thank them all.

Darlene Price offered to help me select departments. Kirsten Farris developed a business plan. Geri Taran came forth and expressed willingness to be our editor. Diana Nichols created our incredible website. Ten other amazing women lent their talents to head up the departments.

Working on the newspaper with Bruce was a wonderful experience. He staged a launch party at *The Gazette* offices for this new section. We had a fabulous turnout.

The section developed to four pages over time. The columns we offered twice monthly included Personal and Professional Development, Business, Health and Wellness, Finance, Community, Volunteerism and Profiles of Accomplished Women. In my column "Personally Speaking", I shared insights on life as I live it. Many of those ideas appear in this book.

Connecting with my readers was one of my most meaningful endeavors. I shared insights and information with many wonderful women who were eager to learn from writers willing to share. Readers gave feedback and appreciation to many of my contributing writers.

The momentum continued throughout the first year. Every now and then, someone who recognized me from my picture would acknowledge me for an article I had written. It wasn't unusual for me to receive an e-mail thanking me for something I wrote that helped them. Often they wrote simply to say "thank you" for creating the section.

To my surprise, several *men* followed my writing and told me that certain articles helped them better understand the women in their lives!

Sadly, our journey together lasted just a little over a year. When the economy slowed down and advertisers cut back on spending, the newspaper closed. Although it had thrived periodically for several years, the stress of making *The Gazette* profitable became too taxing. To my delight, however, it set the stage for what was to later become my writing career.

In my last column, I wrote the following:

I am filled with sadness at the close of a rewarding year. Participating with *The Gazette* opened doors, connected me with readers both in print and on-line, and represented a year of personal and professional growth. I have felt honored and acknowledged every step of the way by your comments, your e-mails and your support. You have shared that many of my "Personally Speaking" columns stimulated change, created new perspectives, and offered a fresh way of looking at an old issue. However my articles may have impacted you, thank you for taking time to include my ideas in your life's journey.

I will miss the challenge of regularly creating "Personally Speaking". I will miss showing up throughout Atlanta with the current *Gazette* under my arm and introducing its value everywhere. I will miss hearing from you. At the same time I'm prepared for new adventures, other avenues to share my insights and for future possibilities . . . Please remember to create the life you want, and the life you deserve. The world needs you and your passion. Declare your determination to be your best self. I so appreciate each of you. (*The Gazette* ~ July, 2001)

While connecting through the printed word was one way to touch people, there are many ways to connect. Find your own way to do so.

The Heart of a Woman

The heart of a woman is an indescribable gift. She initiates conversations with strangers in the bathroom. She recommends the perfect place to find the perfect dress to a woman she meets at the beauty salon. She clips coupons to send to her daughter-in-law. She smiles when she'd rather scream, cries when she's happy, and often says "yes" when her heart wants to say "no." A woman keeps the refrigerator fully stocked in case someone stops by unexpectedly.

A woman aligns with what she believes in by supporting her community with her time and money. She listens to friends, helps with homework, and gives unconditional love. Women cry freely — over their children's accomplishments, during a romantic movie, while reading sentimental cards at a card shop, or when opening a special present. They openly express happiness when hearing about the birth of a baby, an engagement, or a marriage. Women share emotions from their heart.

Women remain strong even when they think they have no strength left. They comfort loved ones in mourning, visit friends and family who are ill, and give hugs and kisses to soothe broken hearts. Simply put, women care! They write letters, make phone calls, send e-mails, and stay in touch. Women connect!

Women do more than give birth. Women are present wherever and whenever they are needed. They intuitively know to offer their love and support. Where a woman is, there is joy and hope. She brings compassion and companionship. She gives moral support. She acknowledges. She reassures.

Women are mothers, daughters, wives, lovers, sisters, aunts, and grandmothers. They give, they guide and they stay grounded. They are amazing not only for what they accomplish, but for the values they impart. Women earn our respect every day, not only because of what they do, but because of who they are.

When you are touched by the heart of a woman, be sure to let her know.

Our "Legends"

Friends remind us of who we are. What would we do without them to mirror back the good we might not see in ourselves? How valuable is it to see the "legends" of who we are in their eyes, to remind us of what we're contributing?

The persona we project to the world may be the person we are striving to become or the mask we are hiding behind. Let's be gentle to ourselves along the way — and be kind to others. After all, each of us is in the process of becoming our true selves.

As we learn, we change. We are influenced by and attracted to others who are also on their journeys. When we associate with people who support us, we have the courage to create our legend.

As we embrace the feedback, we're fortunate to have our wonderful women friends write us thank you notes, care about us, and remind us of how wonderful we are.

As you continue to walk in my boots with me, I'd appreciate it if you'd notice the "Bonnie legend" the world sees before you see the whole, real, not-always-perfect woman on the inside. This woman is still in the process of evolving, bootstep by bootstep.

Create a "Legend" File

We need to keep a file of those thoughtful notes, uplifting statements, and thank yous that we get from time to time. Life hits us with far too many bumps on the head and cuts on the heart for us *not* to need emotional support now and then. There's nothing more wonderful than when I'm having a bad day and I receive a card that says something like the following:

"Bonnie, you walk with a spring in your step and something tells me it's more than just the boots. I first met you at one of those networking events in a large room with everyone holding a stack of business cards in hand. It's like a game. Whoever runs out of cards first wins! I could tell right away you weren't like the hoard of others more interested in handing out cards than in learning about me and my business." *Jane Royal, President of House of Cards (Atlanta)*

"I've watched you, Bonnie, eagerly embrace life and show the rest of us what it's like to live on purpose with great enthusiasm. You thrive on connecting with people. You 'make it happen.' You energize us and set an example. You're a leader! You're a beacon, radiating a huge life force that's on the move, attracting people who see you in action, who sense your mission and want to be a part of it. If they hesitate, they may miss out, because you're *F-A-S-T!* You seize the day! To know you is to feel the energy of connecting, to feel the return of energy back to you, to know there's a positive flow, one woman to another." *Barbara Keddy, President, Be Great! Marketing, Great Falls, VA*

"Happy Birthday, Bonnie. You are valued because you exist in life. Not because you have achieved wealth and are generous with it to various charities. Not because you promote women to gain economic independence. Not because you have worked so diligently and focused to create a harmonious home filled with treasures that delight you and others. BUT just because you ARE. Know you are loved . . ." *Jessica Rareshide, Ideas Strategist, New Orleans, LA*

Isn't that fabulous? I'm so grateful for these friends and for their positive feedback that keeps me going. It helps me see I'm on the right track.

We can all have people in our lives who will do this for us (and who will expect us to do this for them)! Make sure you surround yourself with friends who see the good in you! If all you're hearing is what is wrong with the world or that what you're doing isn't right, rid yourself of that kind of negativity. It may seem difficult at first, but we can phase out the negative people from our lives, replacing them with positive, heart-reassuring people.

You are in the driver's seat. If you're not happy with the direction, change it! If you have non-supportive relationships in your life, connect with new, supportive ones.

To help turn negativity around, go back to your connections.

I encourage you to do something meaningful with your friends — even host a celebratory party. Write a note or record a tape for each other, pretending to be telling someone else about this great person they know — you! You'll be amazed at the value of this type of connection. The impact this will have on those you love and the reinforcement it offers you are priceless.

Feeling Good About Myself

When I feel good about myself
I feel good about you
And good about us.

When I feel good about you
I feel good about myself
And good about us.

When I feel good about us
I feel loved and loving
I feel alive.

Go Where Your Vision Is

"We go where our vision is."
— Joseph Edward Murphy

While they seem the same, there is a huge difference between eyesight and vision. Eyesight is the ability to see what is. Vision is the ability to see the possibilities of what can be.

Today's visions shape tomorrow's opportunities. The strides we make now are the building blocks to what lies ahead.

If you want to see the power of vision in your world, just take a good look at things going on around you. Think about those individuals who have devoted their lives to world peace, knowing that they may not live to see its reality. Look at those in the medical field who continue their research for cures and hold a vision of universal health. What about the educators who devote themselves to eliminating illiteracy? There will always be people committed to a better future because they have the vision to see what's invisible to others.

Yet, look at those visionaries I've mentioned. What do their visions have in common? Each one of them was committed to a vision that led to better lives for others. Each one of them had a vision of a society and a world in which people are helping other people. True visionaries don't visualize a better end only for themselves. Rather, they see a better world.

The Challenge of Visioning

Successful people are colossal dreamers. They can imagine the future and visualize the outcome. They work daily toward their vision.

Visionaries are steadfast in their beliefs and unstoppable in their pursuits. They don't allow the environment, other people's beliefs, or their own limitations to hold them back from their dreams. Only when one ignores the conventional wisdom can he or she achieve the unthinkable.

Had I considered the challenge of writing this book instead of believing in a vision of how my experiences might help someone else, I may have questioned my ability to do so. Moving forward toward uncharted waters when you have faith in a vision creates future possibilities.

People living life by habit refer to it as "same old, same old." People with vision acknowledge change, welcome progress, and expect great results because it's what they expect of themselves.

We can't move forward while standing still. Napoleon Hill, author of *Think And Grow Rich*, stated it best: "Cherish your visions and dreams as they are the children of your soul; the blueprints of your ultimate achievements."

I encourage you to go beyond the reality of what you see at this moment, to your vision of what you wish for the future.

SECTION 7

Connecting Through The Red Door

The Red Door

Women need mentors. From both a practical and a feminine point of view, mentors for women are *it*.

Having come late to the "good ol' boy" networks that men have developed for years, women have had to create their own ways to build relationships in the business world. As women in business have proven themselves to treasure conversation and teamwork, working with mentors seems like a natural thing. It plays right into the powerful traits women possess.

So, what if we created a weekly free mentoring program for professional women! Well, why not?

My friend Kirsten Farris and I developed this idea for entrepreneurs and any women interested in starting a business. We recognized that many women were not getting the support they needed. Existing networking events weren't the right place to support the need for business growth. They are merely a place to exchange business cards.

So we created a mentoring program and called it The Red Door. We met every Tuesday morning at a local Atlanta Bread Company. We occupied a side room. It was a great place to obtain morning coffee and a bagel or pastry. We set up the tables to form a large square and placed chairs around the perimeter. Each participant had five minutes to introduce herself, share with the other women what she does, and give us specific progress on the intention she stated the week before. This format held each person accountable or offered support when life interfered with unmet goals, which was not uncommon! The underlying understanding was that each one of us was there to support, honor, and do what we could to keep every participant on track with their plan. "Red" represented energy and "Door" indicated an opening to the future. Our tag line became "bringing energy to ideas to create unlimited possibilities."

We had no idea that the response would be so great, nor the significance our time and effort would have. Were we in for a surprise! The participation grew weekly. Regulars came faithfully and brought friends. Suddenly we were servicing a large group of entrepreneurial women eager to learn, implement new ideas, and support one another.

From one week to the next, women would report on their previous week's progress and challenges. With the support of their mentors and colleagues, many remained determined to stay on course and strengthen their businesses. We introduced affirmations, spoke our intentions, and encouraged accountability. Women helped each other, and met often between sessions to keep the flow of ideas and momentum going.

Different from other networking groups established for lead generation, The Red Door offered a safe, nurturing space for open dialogue, honest assessment, and a non-threatening environment — perfect for women. For some of our participants, it was their first introduction to mentoring. The Red Door became a foundation for them to go out into the world with their talents, ideas, businesses, and confidence. Kirsten and I know that the contribution of our time, expertise, and connection played a significant role in the success of the women we served. That alone was ample reward.

Talented Businesswoman

Kirsten is an amazing, talented woman. She's brilliant, energetic, and overflows with ideas and enthusiasm as a businesswoman and horse whisperer. She had been in telecommunications sales and marketing for most of her career. She'd moved in and out of the corporate world before starting her own company in 2000. No matter what challenge or question I have, she magically whips up what I need to do or hear. Kirsten takes me under her wing by offering fresh ideas and encouragement. Kirsten and I connected immediately at a luncheon networking function. When I sat down next to her, I asked, "What do you do for fun?" From that one question, Kirsten shared with me her unique perspective on connecting. Here's what she said:

"Really, connecting is not about the questions you ask, because, quite frankly, if someone other than you had asked me 'what do you do for fun?' I might be thinking, I'm not telling this person anything! Just because you ask the question doesn't mean you're going to get the answer! Because I sensed you were genuine, I struck up a conversation."

Yes, connecting is more complicated than it seems. Connecting is not just walking up to another person and striking up a conversation. Before you can connect, you've got to be connected with yourself and your purpose. You have to be genuine.

Discover Your Purpose

How do you discover your purpose? It comes from being aligned with yourself and what you believe in. So how do you get yourself aligned? Therein lies the problem.

We can be very dysfunctional and incongruent. Our conscious minds and our subconscious minds can be out of alignment, out of whack. To find alignment and purpose, we start by discovering our truth and coming into our power. From there, we need to understand that it's all about everybody else. We ask, "How can I help, how can I serve? How can I help people get what they want?"

Connecting is a way of life — not just something you do at meetings, but how you choose to live your life.

To be a connector, you need to be in the realm of helping facilitate transactions between events, people, and things. Get out there, be yourself and be genuine; from there, everything else will fall into place. That's why it's important for people to determine how to get ready.

Kirsten says connection is all there is. In her words, "If you're not connected, you're disconnected. Connection to me is about being abundant and having infinite possibilities. Being disconnected is very limited."

Kirsten feels disconnected at times. She knows that the first step to becoming connected again is to acknowledge feeling disconnected, then getting back in sync.

Do you feel a little depressed? Are you going to do something about it? Do you want to change it? When?

Sometimes, you may want to wallow in the fact that you don't want to do anything at that moment. That's okay, because that's the way energy works. But as Kirsten likes to say, "To make my life work, I have to be in choice. When I choose to do something, I never feel trapped."

It's About Helping Others

Kirsten and I have similar beliefs about networking. We believe it's not about you and it's not about handing out cards. It's about getting to know people and understanding how you can help them. It's about getting to help someone or being involved in a group. You might not get anything tangible from that group, but because you're doing the right thing, good things happen for you. Kirsten and I share that philosophy.

Indeed, true connections are like that. For me, it's nice to find someone like Kirsten who's willing to do things for people because it feels good, and not because she'll get something out of it.

It's a way of life. It's about being open to connect people, and when you do so, you get connected someplace else.

Kirsten says, "You get there by becoming involved in a group similar to The Red Door or *The Joy of Connecting* — by networking with people who are trying to find their purpose and working through exercises that help you determine that purpose. Joining connection groups allows you to just meet and talk with many different people who can steer you onto the right path. Once you're open to it, you just kind of say, 'OK, I'm ready for the next thing — bring it on!' Within 24 hours, great stuff will show up!"

The Horse Whisperer

The joy of connection works for Kirsten in her role as a horse whisperer. Yes, she can actually hold conversations with horses! Well, I'll let her explain the joy of connecting in her life:

"The connecting thing is working for me in my horse world. It's unbelievable! Articles have been written about my being a horse whisperer. It's weird, because when people see me do my thing with the horses, they say, 'You don't look anything like I thought you would.' I dress very businesslike; I drive a nice car. I think they expect some woman to jump out of a van with incense flying! I'm just normal — well, maybe a kind of bridge between the corporate 'real' world and the intuitive world. Everyone who has gotten anywhere is intuitive.

"When I first start 'reading' or talking with horses, and a horse starts telling me its favorite food is a Hardee's biscuit and I tell the owner that, I start thinking 'I must be crazy!' And then when the owner says, 'Oh my gosh, you're totally right. We used to stop by Hardee's and get him a biscuit, and now we don't and he's mad about it.' This is frightening! But I have to go with it. I have to acknowledge it — using intuition and being aware of more — makes life so much easier.

"You know, about a year and a half ago, when I first said, 'I can talk to horses,' I had to go try it! See what happens. So I went to a horse show in Conyers, Georgia. The first person I met was Vickie McTaggert. I said, 'Well if you have a horse here and want me to talk to him, I can.' She said, 'Sure!' I said 'I'll do it for free to show you how this works.'

"Her daughter was in the stable working on the

horse. I went up to it and we talked. Then I told Vickie and her daughter about their horse, that he likes carrots and apples and that he's very businesslike. He wasn't like some horses who are sweet and go up to you — he would never be like that — but he's very honest. I then told her he would be a teacher for their daughter.

"They said, 'Hey, that was really accurate, that was really cool! How much do we owe you?' I declined a fee, but told them if they knew of anyone who might be interested to please refer them to me. About an hour later, they said their trainer, Christy, wanted to meet me! I talked to the other two horses. The end result was that her trainer is now my business partner.

"Talk about a connection! Just from putting myself out there, I met the McTaggerts who introduced me to Christy. From working with Christy and her connections, I've probably read 400 horses in the last year. All of this can be traced back to that one event and that first connection."

I must tell you that when Kirsten and I were doing The Red Door mentoring program, we had an unwritten rule that we only facilitate, not participate. We would give time to others in the group, taking turns and going around the circle. Kirsten and I would mentor and give them the space to express themselves or make the commitment for the next time.

Well, that routine went by the wayside after Kirsten's first experience talking with horses professionally. She came in and said, "I gotta go first!" Even Kirsten, who has her act together, still has to figure things out and wanted mentoring for this new venture. That's what we do for each other and for other people through the joy of connecting.

Connecting With Kristi

I met Kristi Lucariello shortly after she left the corporate arena and went into her own business. She had been a communications director for a company in Orlando and had traveled extensively in the southeast as a regional sales director for another company. Because of those positions, she knew no one in Atlanta when she came here to live.

Kristi, President of Performance in Practice, began her new career as a "success coach" for women. When she got going, she knew she needed to get connected to women. Here's what she said.

"I was very fortunate to meet Bonnie at a special event called Amazing Woman's Day where both of us were speaking. She was just beginning her involvement with eWomenNetwork. When I think about all the connections, all the people she's connected me to, including new clients locally and nationally, I'm astounded.

"I have a coaching, training, and consulting business. I'm a success coach principally with women and so, at the time, I was looking for clients, and looking to build my rolodex. As a coach, I'm not all things to all people. So, one of the things I like to offer my clients is to get them connected to the people and the resources they need."

It's Different in the Corporate World

Through connecting, Kristi has found that relating to people on the outside is quite different from how it works in corporations. She says, "In the corporate world, you're put into this environment and the people you interact with are always there. My experience on the outside is that I get to continually connect and meet new people. These new relationships lead to other new relationships, creating a ripple effect as my contact base grows. While something may not happen right away, the possibility is always there. It's like planting seeds.

"Bonnie's been my role model. There's no question that I've learned how to connect people by watching her and seeing how she creates value. I really didn't have to do that in my corporate job. I really didn't know how.

"Now I get a real kick when I can connect people with one another. When I have clients who need something, I'm pleased that I can provide a way for them to get what they need through networking. I hold a monthly *Girls Nite Out* event and bring in speakers to encourage and help women connect and succeed. How do I get the speakers? Well, one of the things I learned from Bonnie is that all I need to do is ask. Usually they're authors who are happy to share their views through teleconferencing. So I go to the bookstore, find female authors who are interesting, and contact them. I never would have done anything like that before.

"I'm living in this new way of connecting but I'm also showing other women how to do the same for themselves. I use the word collaborate more now than I have in my entire life. It's not about competition. It's about how we can collaborate. How can we do something together? How can I help you? And, maybe you can help me."

Seeds Grow and Flowers Blossom

Kristi has found connecting to be the key to a business that is better than she ever expected. She ties this success to all the seeds she's planted along the way — all the connections she's made.

"For example, a woman I met over a year ago called me and said she's ready for coaching. I'm also working with some coaches who are like-minded. I'm working with a local author who is very collaborative. I also have a client in California whom Bonnie introduced me to. She's starting a virtual university concept for CPAs, accountants, and small-business people. She's had to be collaborative in getting her project up and running. I've shared a lot of resources with her and just the other day I asked *her* for a resource.

"As a coach, I'm also not the one that needs to be in the limelight. I'm the one in the background cheering my clients on who need to be in the limelight. I love the whole idea of collaboration — connecting people. That's why I fit in so well because that's who I am and what I do."

Kristi has become a role model for others to learn how effective connecting can be in our lives. She has begun offering a weekly mentoring group similar to what we've been doing with The Red Door. They meet weekly, giving women an opportunity to come together to share, learn from each other, and get the support they need for their individual endeavors.

She also demonstrates what she calls "prosperity thinking." As Kristi says, "If you are in the competition mode and don't want to give out names, you are demonstrating the flip side of connecting and collaborating. There are so many people out there with whom we can connect. We couldn't possibly tap all the resources or diminish them. There are more than enough opportunities to go around."

I just love the "prosperity thinking" concept — a new

way of being. I love that my Red Door mentoring group is being replicated by Kristi. It all inspires me. Until we connect, we have *no idea* the effect we can have on one another when we come from a place of abundance rather than depletion! Connecting is *not* work. It's something one *wants* to do. It feels right to want to be a person who takes delight in sharing.

Connecting With Bonnie

During the research for this book, I spoke with dozens of women who have connected through the endeavors my colleagues and I have undertaken. I am humbled by their stories and the way they say I have influenced their lives.

The stories that follow are heartfelt examples of the power and the joy of connecting.

Laura Biering

Laura Biering is a certified coach, an ordained priestess who performs ceremonies for individuals who don't have a traditional affiliation and she also teaches the Artist's Way. Her company is called True Voice, Inc. When we met, she was just getting started on the coaching side of her career and found her way to The Red Door.

Although Laura possesses an operatic voice, it had been close to seven years since she'd sung in public. Personal challenges had stripped her of her "voice" and she was reluctant to bring it out for others to hear. The last time she had sung was at her grandmother's funeral, deeply touching those assembled when she sang "Amazing Grace."

For Laura, The Red Door came at a time when she needed to take herself to the next level of professionalism. Although she could call on a lot of people for support, her participation included holding her accountable for intentions that made it worthwhile. At The Red Door, she felt challenged, nurtured, and loved.

Martha Lanier

Martha Lanier, whose company is called Ignite Your Potential, is a member of the National Speakers Association. She says, "Bonnie and I met almost three years ago. I was impressed with her when we first connected. She showed confidence, demonstrated professionalism, and seemed eager to meet other women and grow her contact base. I had no idea until much later that she was just starting her own career path. She portrayed a demeanor that was positive and spoke with an established presence."

This is the story of how connecting changed her life.

"My life has changed dramatically since March of 2000. That was when Bonnie staged the Amazing Women Day at a mall in Atlanta. It was at this event that I first agreed to speak in public. I had just started a coaching career but did not know that I could speak professionally. After that, I would periodically run into Bonnie at a local networking event. I was green, and she was a familiar face. We would catch up with one another at Ben & Jerry's Ice Cream Parlor and one day we met each other's spouses. As we shared where we each lived, it turned out we were almost neighbors, which was a bonus.

"Bonnie told me about a group she represented, eWomenNetwork, but because I was working full-time and developing my speaking career and coaching part-time, my schedule was packed. Some time later, I did attend my first eWomenNetwork meeting and Bonnie was there. I was immediately drawn to her. She has subsequently become a dear friend, exemplifying ease and generosity — a rare thing. She's a magnet. Some people are pushy — not Bonnie — she is supportive. She had persevered by sending out an e-mail once a month just saying,

'I think you'd enjoy coming' and I finally did!

"As of January, I had left the controlled environment of the corporate world. My husband was an independent contractor. I wanted my own company, but didn't know how. I had to get out of my comfort zone. So on my 50th birthday, I went to learn skydiving!

"I'm now doing what *I* love! I'm working to build *my* dreams — what I am passionate about. Two years ago I was petrified. Today I finally get to speak about it. I told myself there was no way I'd have my own company and be incorporated! Skydiving changed my mindset. I went home and told our children they could do anything and do it well.

"After participating with Bonnie at eWomen Network, she introduced me to Freedom Builders and to more opportunities. Her introductions later produced speaking engagements and coaching clients.

"I learned from Bonnie *not to sit at home, but to get out and be giving.* While I realized how much our lives intertwined, I also knew we have to put forth the effort to get the results we are looking for.

"I believe in connecting. I met more people in one year than I had in my entire lifetime. Now when I enter a room, I greet everyone there. I believe we can become more successful if we're not alone. Through connections and becoming involved, doors open! Everything we do or say has a ripple effect. We are a part of something bigger than ourselves if we choose not to be isolated."

Ann Preston

Ann Preston is the Founder/Creator of Freedom Builders, a networking and connecting group. She is a true entrepreneur.

When she started her organization, approximately 12 of us met in the back room of a restaurant. From that humble beginning, the number of participants at each subsequent meeting increased. Before long, what started out as a free "get-together" became a full-fledged members-only organization with meetings all over Greater Atlanta. I was invited to her first gathering and, to this day, I feel proud to be a part of this organization. Here's her story.

"Bonnie and I first met at Power Core, a national membership organization. In a way, we were 'competitors' and it was a little rough in the beginning. We were two women who both thought they knew how they wanted to do things. It took me a while to realize she really wanted my organization to be a player with hers. Here, she was 'recruiting' for eWomenNetwork and I was 'recruiting' for Freedom Builders. But she wanted me to join eWomen so the women who were members would also have Freedom Builders as an additional resource for contacts and business development.

"I observed that guests and members alike catered to Bonnie whether she was leading an eWomenNetwork meeting or participating as a member of Freedom Builders. I watched with amazement and interest. Whether they were experienced or nervous, one hundred percent of the participants looked at Bonnie while they were telling about themselves and their services. She made that vital connection with them because she listened so actively. It was the most powerful thing! She became one of our first members.

"I realized then and there I would use the 'BRP (Bonnie Ross-Parker) Approach' — you can have the world if you care! — in Freedom Builders. This is a huge concept. Consequently, I listen to new members. The results are phenomenal. I get e-mails all the time from people saying they used to be so uncomfortable networking, but now they want to come 'because *you're* there. I feel there is someone there who cares for me, someone genuine.'

"I had a sense of that but didn't know how to express it. Yet that approach *changed the course of my company*. Now it is becoming more of a natural ability for me.

"As I look back to when we first connected, I think Bonnie didn't view us as competitors. That may have been my perception and therefore I reacted cautiously. I think the turning point came when I went to her eWomen group for the first time. That evening I was exhausted. I had been doing Freedom Builders all day and I was disheveled, starving. Suddenly, so many people were coming up to me. They kept saying they knew who I was, treating me like a celebrity! I felt famous!

"Bonnie can be a tough mentor. For example, she was teaching me about *keeping your word*. One time, I was invited to be a guest at her cocktail party. I was so busy, I didn't go. I didn't call, thinking *nobody will notice if I'm not there*. But she called me!

"'Where were you? I was worried! Never break your word. Let the person know. It's very important for your reputation in business.' She made me feel awful. I got it! But it wasn't about 'you were bad.' It was that she *cared*.

"Bonnie says we're a perfect fit now — two powerfully-minded women working together, supporting each other openly. I couldn't be happier! A lot of women I connect with and care about are younger than I am. We're doing great things! When we get these high level, like-minded women together, sparks fly! We foresee in the future the possibilities are limitless.

"I've been an entrepreneur for 15 years, and have been taking courses with big organizations. What I see is people living in a box. But many are breaking out with the help of Freedom Builders and The Joy of Connecting. We accelerate the process for them to find their *passion*. Be a mentor like Bonnie, who says, 'If you don't share the belief yet, borrow mine.' It's instantaneous — people grow before your very eyes! Take a stranger and guide them, reach out to them and mentor them."

Illona Cardona

Illona Cardona is a milliner who also found her way through The Red Door. Here's her story:

"Every now and then, one experiences a really wonderful feeling of being a part of something bigger than oneself! That's the feeling I got from The Red Door.

"Bonnie Ross-Parker and Kirsten Farris helped us see the possibilities of what we needed to do to go to the next step. They were mothers when we needed them, mentors always, expert networkers and most of all supporters of our dreams and ambitions!

"It was wonderful being a part of this group! I met women all striving to become better at the tasks at hand and most importantly, willing to share experiences and challenges to grow as women in business. Having been in business for several years but struggling to re-open my store, I had the opportunity to help those through my experiences, frustrations, and opportunities and learn valuable lessons as well.

"It's a very powerful thing to see people work together for a common goal, to experience the strength that comes from belonging and the love that is shared. I believe some of the relationships I made there will last a lifetime.

"Having been a part of The Red Door, I have since become involved with other women's business networks. I am a member of The Northern Entrepreneurial Women (NEW) with Carole Madan, Georgia Women in Networking (GA-WIN) with Sara Im. I was a conference speaker at Georgia Women's Entrepreneurial Network (GWEN), an outreach of the Georgia State University in Athens. I am a frequent attendee of the Atlanta Womens Network meetings and Atlanta Business Women Association. The Red Door showed me the power of networking.

"The Red Door is closed now and we have gone our ways, separate and together. But we'll always remember what The Red Door opened for women entrepreneurs willing to share for the common good of all."

Latching on to a Support System

Thalia Autry and I met at a point in her life when hope was the furthest thing from her mind. We connected at a mentoring group sponsored by GRASP, a nonprofit organization that supports the entrepreneurial endeavors of low-income women in metro-Atlanta. Thalia had come to GRASP to learn how to write a business plan for her newly formed business, The Corporate Key. A single mom, she wanted to work from home so she could better manage her home life and have more time for her five children.

She had just lost a good job, been abandoned by a drug-using, wife-abusing husband, and had lost her home to foreclosure. To sum it up, she was alone, unemployed, penniless, and technically homeless. Her children often went hungry and she was able to offer them nothing but rice. But she came through it all. Thalia explains:

"Bonnie epitomized hope to me. Before meeting her, I had no support system for my new endeavor. I had no idea what I was doing. I just knew from recent readings that *I was not a victim* and could *create my future according to my wishes*. I was standing in a strange place, and the truth is that I was terrified.

"Bonnie soothed me. She noticed me because I was reading Napoleon Hill's book *Think and Grow Rich*. I didn't realize that she was to be the speaker that evening, but I noticed her because her aura was very bright and her spirit felt warm, friendly, and safe to me. Once the evening began, she explained to the group that the entrepreneurial journey required vision, strength, support, and perseverance. It was all about delay and not denial. She encouraged us to show up, not give up, and to seek a support system. She explained an 'elevator pitch' and its importance in selling services.

"She asked each of us about our businesses with genuine interest. She told me she liked the concept of The Corporate Key, which encouraged me simply because she understood. Although she spoke to a group of us, I felt like she was talking only to me. That night, Bonnie provided the sign that I was on the right track.

"After attending The Red Door, so much happened to me. Because of the elevator speech that I learned there, I met a woman named Alice Bussey, co-owner of Bussey Florist in Decatur. Ms. Bussey invited me to participate in the Atlanta Business League (ABL), where I am a member of the membership committee and chair of the Administrative subcommittee. In the committee and the group, I have made even more connections. I work closely with Ms. Bussey, who has influential connections throughout metro-Atlanta. I manage administrative work for her in the way that The Corporate Key intends. Working with her has given me the opportunity to make other business connections and expose the quality of my work to important people in a low-risk environment. In essence, Ms. Bussey is my mentor.

"I also got to know Kirsten Farris, who helped me financially, to study for the CPA exam, develop a time line calendar, and organize steps that would lead me to take the CPA exam.

The Connections Keep Coming

Thalia continues. . . .

"Illona Cardona and I met at GRASP, but our connection didn't solidify until The Red Door. Initially, I was going to help her with six years of taxes she needed prepared. With my assistance, she was able to turn a liability that was in the thousands to a return of about $1,500.

"Illona helped me on a numerous occasions, too. She bought my family a Christmas tree, Christmas decorations, and gifts. While I was trying to meet an important deadline, she and the children put the tree up, decorated it, and sang Christmas carols. They called me for the official tree lighting. She turned an otherwise drab holiday into one that the kids remember with joy.

"I made connections with Cleopatra Bell, Mary Bob Straub, Juanita Bellavance, and Kristi Lucariello. Cleopatra and I met at The Red Door, but we really began to talk after we ran into each other at the Five Points MARTA station. We're working on a 40-Day Prosperity Plan, detailed in *The Abundance Book* by John Randolph Price. She checks on me almost every day. She and I attend the WE Success Group, which is another mentoring support group.

"Mary Bob and I have encouraged each other during different phases in our journey. Juanita and I, with two other women, are forming a mastermind group to leverage each other's efforts to become multi-millionaires. She is also one of the people editing my book *Doing Small Business the Big Business Way.*

"Kristi founded the WE Success Group. Cleopatra learned about Kristi through Bonnie and invited me to the group once The Red Door ended. Because of Kristi, who focuses on internal work, I have committed to healing myself in addition to building my business and writing my book.

"I could go on and on, but I think that I have made

my point clear. Making connections is pertinent to successful change. By making connections, I have expanded my awareness and leveraged my ability exponentially. When I started, my life was in an upheaval. Now, I have a well-defined business. Even though I am not completely out of the woods, I am well on my way to the life that I have envisioned.

"I believe the positive energy of the connections aided me in attracting the right people into my life. Overall, I attribute the changes in my life to the well-defined support system that I was able to build because of The Red Door and Bonnie Ross-Parker. She orchestrated the connections that I needed to improve my life and for that, and much more, I thank her."

SECTION 8

Disconnections

eWomenNetwork

Around the time *The Gazette* column was ending, I made a new connection for a new opportunity. It was another example of keeping myself "out there" even while being immersed in something else.

I received a call out of the blue from a colleague excited to share ideas about a project he and his wife were developing. We had worked together on a different venture and he had followed my success at the newspaper (the women's section was a success even though the newspaper closed). He wanted to know if I'd be interested in finding out more about his venture.

They were launching a new concept in women's membership organizations. They wanted to create a large membership-based and Internet-based organization for women called *eWomenNetwork*. The Internet site would showcase the organization's members and give women global exposure to expand their products and services.

It didn't surprise me that they contacted me, as much as I love connecting women with each other, and it certainly appeared congruent with what I was already doing. I said "yes" to being a member and became a marketing representative. With assurance that I'd be part of eWomenNetwork's long-range plan, I jumped in, heart and soul — a venture that began as a total love affair.

Within 18 months, I sponsored more members and brought in more revenue for the organization than any other representative. I hosted local networking events every month. I brought on board several premier faculty members who presented at various functions year round. Many exciting things were happening for so many women because of this.

One of the women I met was Jane Royal. Her story is a prime example of what we were doing at eWomenNetwork.

"Like most things in my life, I started my graphic design business after months of carefully thought-out dreaming. I didn't have a formal 'plan.' I just had years of experience, some talent, and an open mind. I attended a conference in May of 2001 and in the 'goodie bag' of handouts, I found a purple half-sheet with a friendly invitation to have breakfast and meet other women entrepreneurs. I had no idea what was waiting for me.

"WOW! What started out as an ordinary Saturday will always be remembered as a turning point in my life. When I walked into the room, Bonnie greeted me and asked about my graphic design business. I felt right at home.

"I mingled, meeting the other women entrepreneurs of all ages and types. I felt as if I *belonged* there! These women, all so different, were all very much the same: We were determined to have our own businesses and earn a living on our terms. I could feel the power of that energy in the room. We were all here. Bonnie's mission and the mission of eWomenNetwork was to *support all of us*.

"Before I left that meeting, I had one new client. The next time I attended, Bonnie hired me to design *her* business card. The days and weeks that followed were a blur of phone calls, meetings, and new business. The best part: I was helping eWomen with its branding efforts and through that, I was growing my own business. The magic had begun. After six years of waiting, I was living the dream.

"I discovered another wonderful side to eWomen

when an emergency arose. My sister-in-law, pregnant with twins, was having complications. My husband was out of town and I had just learned that the babies would be born four months premature! If they lived, there was a long list of problems that could occur.

"I turned to my eWomen friends and received an out-pouring of support, encouraging words, and prayers. Some of these women I had only known for a few weeks, but they were right there for me. The relationships that have spawned from those days are like a steady stream of gifts. My networking circle and my client base grow larger every day. It's all about giving and passionately connecting people."

Disconnections

I was part of eWomenNetwork early in its develop-ment and played a significant role in its growth. The ease with which I sponsored new members and retained exist-ing members made this venture personally and financially rewarding.

By my second year, the number of members had increased substantially and, unfortunately, with that growth several challenges surfaced. In spite of my best efforts, my ideas weren't accepted, leading to great frustra-tion on my part. It became clear that what I had thought was going to be a long-term, protected future with this company was over. I felt my value diminished and my issues ignored. We parted ways after 18 months.

When eWomenNetwork closed its door to me (or did I close the door to it?), I felt totally abandoned. Having given so much of myself to the company, constantly singing its praises, and putting time and energy into ensur-ing its success, it was painful for me to let go. I had allowed myself to get totally caught up in the excitement, expansion, and vision. At the time it felt like home. I belonged. I had a future. eWomenNetwork lived in my heart.

I thrived on learning about and participating in the company's developments. The CEO, her husband, and Phil and I became very close. They stayed with us during their Atlanta visits. We spoke daily. Promises were made. The connection the four of us felt was strong and endearing. I never imagined that we would part ways. While I had no contract and was specifically commissioned, I had every reason to believe that as my contribution increased, so would my compensation.

Yet, slowly, differences in opinions about policies and practices arose between us. During the early stages of the endeavor, they sought my opinion, and my feedback seemed relevant. We'd talk for hours about changes they wanted to implement, and I felt confident to voice my acceptance when I agreed, and my concerns when I didn't.

In addition, I participated with a small group of eWomenNetwork members who had reached the highest pay plan, as I had. We stayed in touch to compare notes, share our successes, and support each other. The five of us became very close. We envisioned both a long-standing connection with the company and with one another.

However, our close relationship and the ideas we brought forward didn't sit well with our CEO. Behaviors that seemed collaborative and cooperative at the onset were viewed as destructive and distrustful. It became a "them versus us" situation. While I had chosen not to participate in either corporate America or a political arena, I suddenly found myself dealing with both. It became clear I was working *for* a company, not *with* it. I was extremely disappointed and upset over this turn of events.

While I never saw my role as *only* a commissioned representative, the reality hit me hard. That's exactly what I was. I had no official voice. I had no influence. However, I did have a choice. I could stay and work the system as dictated or I could make my exit.

As I became more frustrated with the executives of eWomenNetwork, they became more hostile toward me. The dream of staying on forever and having a place with the company became an illusion. I knew it was only a matter of time. One more unpleasant conversation or one more mandate would make me walk. As it turned out, they called the question and *invited* me to leave.

Dealing with the Post-Mortem

What went wrong? What happened? How did we go from being close and connected to being estranged and disconnected?

I've thought a lot about the joy that being part of eWomenNetwork brought to my life. I've thought about the heartbreak. I've searched within for the lessons I needed to learn and for the role I played in our parting ways. While I still don't have all the answers, I do know that we each benefited from the journey we shared, however short it lasted. I connected with women I would not have met otherwise. I proved to myself that I had value in the workplace.

I can recall some great experiences and important lessons. Like any other journey, each one is a stepping-stone to the next. I just never expect journeys to end. I think they should continue forever. As it turned out, eWomenNetwork went in one direction and I chose another. *Walk In My Boots* has become my new journey.

I tell this story not to say that eWomenNetwork was a bad idea — it wasn't! We connected with so many women, most of whom have better and more fulfilling lives because of it. But sometimes, no matter how good the intentions, a project or an initiative just doesn't work out. This one didn't work out for me.

Disconnections happen. We begin with great intentions, do fine work, and something goes wrong — they don't appreciate us, things get in the way, we're called to another purpose.

Connecting is not only about connecting with others. It's also about connecting with ourselves. We must be strong enough and honest enough to admit when something is not working and declare that it's time to move on. We are of no help to others if we are not happy or comfortable ourselves.

Whose fault was the disconnection at eWomen Network? It really doesn't matter who was to blame, or if there was any blame to pass around. What matters is that sometimes things break. Disconnections simply happen.

We need to accept that and deal with it. Someone once said, "When one door closes, God opens a window." When we feel disconnected and the door seems to be closed, we just might feel a breeze behind us.

The eWomenNetwork was a catalyst in my decision to write this book. With so much experience related to connecting, and the value that connecting offers to those who implement connecting as a way of *being*, I knew the time was right to begin this *new journey*. I could pursue this endeavor unencumbered. There was no turning back.

Silence

Sometimes when we are together, silent
There is love and sharing
In the unspoken words.

Sometimes when we are together, silent
I feel distant and alone.

Then, yesterday's intimacy is hiding.
Are you also lonely?
Please
Talk to me.

Judgments Not Allowed

In the 1800s, Walt Whitman said, "Be curious, not judgmental." Unfortunately, judgment comes because most of us see ourselves as the center of the universe.

When we are quick to judge others, we really put labels on them based on our own perception of what we consider appropriate. We might find fault with someone else's hairstyle, way of dressing, conduct, kind of work, and so on. Statements like, "I can't believe she bought that car!" and "Did you notice the way he treated his son?" and "How could anyone that overweight eat dessert?" indicate we're judging another's behavior. What gives us the right to do that?

Know that when you judge others, you don't define *them*, you only define yourself. You're entitled to make your own choices in whatever way they serve you. All judgments are based on what *you* think. Just as *you* have control over rejecting another's judgment of you, it's essential to give others the same right.

Use your best judgment in every situation. Allow others to do what seems right to them. When you look at the moon, you see only part of it, yet you know there's a much larger object there. In the same way, when you look at or communicate with someone, you glimpse through only a partial window into that person's life. People are much more than their appearances or their dialogues. For you to judge them on what's obvious is to obliterate all that's possible and hidden from view. It's more compassionate to honor people not by how they look or what they say, but rather by what's in their hearts.

Authentic communication in any relationship happens when you eliminate judgment. All participants are free to think, to express themselves, to engage in what serves them best, to make their own decisions, and to live life without external limitations. Imagine a world in which participants engage life to their fullest potential, feel unencumbered, treat one another with dignity, and serve society for the greater good of everyone.

When we stop judging others and begin *respecting them completely*, we'll create a better world for us all.

Agree to Disagree

I'll admit it. It's difficult for me to handle a point of view different from my own when the situation at hand seems obvious to me.

How do you remain neutral and unemotional? Remaining neutral has to be a conscious decision. It requires unconditionally accepting someone else's opinion regardless of what I think or how I feel. Yet the closer I am to a situation, the harder it is to maintain neutral. This is *especially* true with family and close friends.

How do you stay neutral when tough issues such as the care of aging parents, your adult children's parenting skills, career and relationship choices, money, religion and politics come to the table? These topics by their very nature evoke strong opinions. How well siblings deal with problems affecting their parents can have a major impact on their relationships with each other in the long term. Being judgmental about a best friend's choice of life partner can ruin what appeared to be a close friendship. Who could possibly think that any discussion with differing opinions around heated issues during an election year could be harmonious?

Can anyone know what is best for another individual? What does it take to agree to disagree?

Disagree in Harmony

A good place to start is to be totally open-minded. This means listening without judgment, interruption, or strategizing. It means not thinking of the next thing you're going to say while the other person is still talking or explaining. It means paying attention. It requires asking questions. It demands honoring and respecting the reality that each of us responds to life and circumstances in different ways. Our opinions and judgments are created from these experiences and previous encounters.

Someone else's point of view is neither right nor wrong; it just is.

While this may sound simple, we don't operate that way in the real world. We often seem quick to respond, eager to jump in with our point of view, or even worse, ready to dismiss another's idea by quickly replacing it with our own. Imagine the harmony that could take place if people would accept that disagreeing is healthy and normal. Imagine viewing our differences as assets instead of liabilities. Imagine settling disagreements based on *facts* instead of *emotions*. Of course, this requires removing our egos and replacing "self" with objectivity.

What price do we pay when we diminish someone else because we demand to be right? What value is gained by being narrow-minded and inflexible? What new understandings can we create by respectfully allowing ourselves and others to disagree?

The next time you face a situation that demands self-restraint during open dialogue, consider the outcome you want beforehand. Decide if you want to have a clearer view or to close the window. After all, *you* control how you act, what you say, and what attitude you show. You have a choice. Either choose to disagree or choose to be determined to win regardless of the cost. Both choices are a reflection of your character.

Agree to disagree and "be" what you want the world to see.

If Only

How many *if onlys* do you have in your life?

If only I had moved when I could have. *If only* I had listened to my parents' advice. *If only* I hadn't been so eager to quit my job. *If only* I had given the decision more careful consideration. *If only* I had taken care of my health. *If only* I had spent more time with my family. *If only, if only, if only.*

If only is a way of looking back with regret over what we did or didn't do. We wish we had handled a certain outcome differently. But what a waste of time, energy, and thinking! Instead of focusing on *if only*, consider what we could gain by embracing them as life lessons!

Some of us look back and label each performance either as a success or failure. Imagine how different you'd feel if you changed your point of view and acknowledged that those experiences that did not turn out the way you wanted were steppingstones for growth. What if you acknowledged that whatever happened at that time in your life was meant to happen? What if you could only do what you could do based on your knowledge and experience at the time? What if you accepted that you could not make other decisions because you didn't know the things you found out when all was said and done?

We make choices based on the knowledge we have, not on the knowledge we're going to have. We listened or didn't listen to our parents because we knew that we needed to make our own decisions, no matter what the outcome. We quit jobs because our knowledge tells us there's something better, or maybe that we're bored. We did or didn't take care of our health based on how we felt when we were younger.

Your decisions never exist in a vacuum. They're based on everything that's going on in your life at the time you make each one.

If only I had written this book sooner. If only I had left eWomenNetwork sooner.

If only . . .

Progress in our lives is possible when we learn from the past and don't lament over what we wish we'd done!

SECTION 9

Re-connecting . . .
with Yourself

A Surprise: The Shadow Behind the Smile

I felt at the peak — doing things I'd never achieved before, making remarkable connections for colleagues, seemingly at the height of my power. I was the woman everyone wanted to be with, a woman of impact!

Yet, I felt vulnerable. I just wanted to be who I was. But who *was* I?

I am passionate and committed. I am fragile and strong. I am focused and uncertain. I need to give. I need to receive. I need to cheerlead. I need cheering. I need to express myself. I need others to share with me. I love myself. I am the connector.

At a certain point in my life, I was needing validation from others. I recognized the vivacious woman behind the confident smile occasionally felt left out.

Am I always the bridesmaid and never the bride? I have spent the major part of my adult life honoring and supporting everybody else's journeys. I plug in, light up, and ignite those who benefit from my energy. But what about Bonnie? Where are my tangible rewards? What is the legacy I'm leaving?

Many women who give so much to others also feel this way from time to time, especially when they don't think their efforts are being reciprocated. In my case, there was reciprocity but sometimes it just wasn't apparent. For me, making that discovery and acknowledging it took many years to come into my consciousness.

In the meantime, I would thrive on these doubts, these needs for reassurance, these feelings of vulnerability because they came at the perfect time: the time to write this book. Writing led me on an inner journey of evaluation and discovery — a road into the past and present with family and self. It was not an easy road to take, but it's been oh, so enlightening to pave the way for reconnections and new connections.

Make "Time for You" Time

Ever wonder if there will ever be time for just *you?*

As women, we manage many tasks, wear many hats, and get involved in a multitude of activities. Sometimes, when the day ends, I just keep going. When I finally have the opportunity to do something just for me, I'm too tired to think about it. Something is wrong with this picture!

I challenge you to pick up a women's magazine that *doesn't* address the value of making time for yourself. Ads invite you to treat yourself to a day at the spa, to take a long, luxurious bath with candles while listening to soothing music, to visit the beach, or take a pleasure trip. I wonder how many women *really* take time to do the things they deserve. Do you?

For me, the real issue is priorities. How can I fulfill the constant demands on my time, delegate or eliminate the things I do because I've always done them, and provide a window of time that's flexible and fulfilling just for me? What price does my mental and physical well-being pay when I don't put "me" time on my list? The reality is that if I don't make myself a priority, no one else will.

A wise person once said that we create, promote, or allow everything in our lives. We have control. If there is something we don't like, we have the choice to change it because we're in the driver's seat of our life's journey. That being said, I constantly take time to re-evaluate my schedule and re-prioritize my activities.

I choose to feel good about myself, to be worthy of indulgences every now and then, and to eliminate the feelings of guilt when I say "no" to the world's demands and "yes" to my own needs. I am making a commitment to take time for me.

I encourage you to do the same.

Self-Love

Have you ever been stuck in a place where you didn't feel smart enough, thin enough, creative enough, loving, confident, worthy, or just plain ok? Well, I have. I can remember being at parties and feeling inappropriately dressed. I can recall going to social events and having nothing to say. There have been times at networking events when everyone seemed engaged in conversation and I had to inch my way into a circle of people to appear less self-conscious.

I can remember comments from family members that felt like criticism. One comment in particular happened over three decades ago and still sits in my head as if it were yesterday.

At the time, my two children were five and two years old, and with my then-husband's support, I decided to return to teaching. We made all the necessary arrangements and the schedule was working out to everyone's benefit. My daughter was in kindergarten and my son stayed with a grandmother who cared for three other children. The school I worked at was nearby, so all of us were in the same neighborhood.

During one particular family gathering, my sister-in-law, a stay-at-home mom, pulled me aside to ask me this: "I'm just curious. How do you think you can be an effective mom if you're working full time? I would think motherhood would be rewarding enough. Maybe you're just not as happy as I am being a mom?"

I honestly don't remember what I said in response to her comment, but our relationship was never the same after that. I had initially felt confident in my decision to balance work and family. But after my sister-in-law's remarks, I had to muster the resolve to believe in myself and know that what I was doing was best for us all. At the time, my self-confidence took a real nosedive.

It's taken a lot of hard work to finally come to a place in my life where I feel self-confident and self-assured. It's unlikely you can really connect with others when you don't feel connected with yourself. The question becomes, "How does one connect with oneself?"

The "I am 100's List"

For me, achieving self-acceptance was a gradual process. As an avid reader, I became a student of personal development.

Over the years, I have read many self-help, motivational books. I experienced a significant breakthrough to self-acceptance after developing a friendship with a wonderful woman, Linda Larsen, who taught me an exercise I still do.

Referred to as the "I am 100's List" it is a process whereby you literally affirm your greatness twice a day. Here's what you do. You generate a list of 100 qualities that you possess. It's not important that you demonstrate any specific quality *all the time*. As long as you have *ever* possessed the quality, you deserve to claim it!

I found it easiest to do this alphabetically. For example, "I am awesome," "I am authentic," "I am brave," "I am beautiful," "I am caring," "I am confident," "I am capable," "I am deserving," etc.

Generate the list until you get to 100 qualities!

I decided to be kind to myself ("I am kind") and affirm qualities that I desired, even if I didn't *really* believe they were accurate descriptors of me. Deep down, I knew I possessed lots of wonderful attributes, although sometimes I didn't *feel* worthy to acknowledge them. Isn't that like each of us? We are often as afraid of our strengths as we are of our weaknesses ("I am worthy").

Sit down and write your list. After it's completed, read the list aloud twice a day. It is good practice to read it as your day begins and as you retire in the evening. I take a copy of my list with me in the car so when I am caught in traffic, I can re-affirm, "I am patient!" "I am accepting!"

After reading my list for a while, I began to feel differently about myself. I began to *feel* stronger. I began to *feel* brave. I began to *feel* worthy. As I gave myself permission to be self-assured, I *felt* assured. This exercise helped me clear my self-doubt. I became more loving and accepting of myself and others. I let go of the illusion of perfection ("I'm ok"), and allowed myself to be human ("I am human"). Simultaneously, I found myself behaving in ways that were more loving toward others ("I am loving").

It's as if I wanted to do more to acknowledge people because I knew from my own experience that we don't get acknowledged and appreciated nearly as much as we deserve. By acknowledging myself through the "I am 100's List," it significantly lessened my need to hear it from the outside. At the same time, the exercise increased my desire to connect and affirm the joy I felt from within with others.

I bet I know what you're thinking: "There's *no way* something that simple can produce the results you're talking about!" The truth is, it *does*. Acknowledging yourself brings you the inner joy you deserve and fills you with greatness. It creates overflowing peace and encourages you to instill it in others. Remember Muhammad Ali's repeated phrase, "I'm the greatest!" I believe his affirmation — speaking his truth over and over again — did promote his greatness from the inside out.

Who you are in the world and how you project yourself determines the degree to which others are attracted to you. When you show the world your confident self ("I am confident"), it's easy to connect with other people. As they connect with and admire you, it inspires you to continue being a self-assured individual. As your self-confidence develops and strengthens, so, too, will your relationships. Being self-confident has to be an inside job. *No one* can do that for you.

Reading self-help books, listening to motivational tapes, and faithfully reading aloud the "I am 100's List" twice daily all inspired me to create and teach the concepts behind the joy of connecting. While I had been connecting over a lifetime, I didn't develop the passion to help others believe in themselves until I first *learned to believe in myself.*

Today, I trust my talents ("I am talented") and I love listening to the stories others share, to support the needs they express, and to offer encouragement. I *know* the value connection has for us all.

When you feel great about yourself, you can't help but want the same well-being for others. That's why your delivering a kind word, offering a compliment, remembering someone during a time of crisis, being generous, listening, and allowing someone else to benefit because of who you are is such a high. While another's appreciation of you may not be expressed, your kindness will never be forgotten. You *know the feeling* when others acknowledge you. When you give the gift of that feeling to others over and over again, you, too, will feel the inner joy that comes from being a person who connects.

Add "I am connected" to your list!

Applaud Your Success

Why do I rely on others giving me credit for what I accomplish instead of giving myself credit? There are times when I get so much done that at the end of the day, I've amazed myself. When that happens, I still find myself wondering, "Does anyone even notice all that I do?"

With this in mind, I decided to keep track of my successes and acknowledge myself! I am an avid journalist. Writing helps me identify what I am thinking, feeling, accomplishing, and the areas in which I need to focus. When I write I can express myself fully and appreciate where I've been. It's my time and my space to get in touch with myself in an unencumbered arena. In the privacy of my mind, I allow myself the sheer pleasure of saying "yes" to myself, all that I am, and what I strive to be.

Do you keep "to do lists" and check off the things you finish? Do you "multi-task" all day long? Do you "juggle" your schedule between work and family and create personal time? If you do, applaud yourself!

On the many days when I eat healthy, I frequently forget to acknowledge myself for making great choices. I do seem to berate myself for not being more conscientious after those times when I eat a rich dessert (although I know better) or decide not to exercise (because I'm not in the mood). There's something inherently unfair about focusing on what I didn't do rather than giving myself credit for what I accomplish — especially when I know I consistently eat healthy and exercise regularly!

I bet you can think of lots of examples in your life when you forgot to focus on your successes and dwelled on your shortcomings instead. Do you applaud those times when you remember to send a card, buy a gift, or acknowledge someone? Do you give yourself credit when you plan and execute a terrific dinner party, even if you inadvertently left something in the refrigerator? Do you congratulate yourself when you stay on schedule and keep your commitments?

We deserve to be recognized for the many things we do, the tasks we accomplish, and the contributions we make. Everyone is so busy doing what they *need* to do that many of their accomplishments go unnoticed.

We know the feeling of pride in successfully fulfilling our responsibilities. We also know the effect others have when they produce a positive result.

As you begin the process of applauding your successes (and not waiting for others to do it for you), I suggest you also take the time to applaud others' successes. Remind them they deserve to be acknowledged and appreciated. Encourage them to give themselves credit for their positive decisions and accomplishments. After all, every one of us benefits from focusing on our successes.

Your Ideas Matter

Every time you share your ideas, you bring value to others. Ideas come in many forms. It can be as simple as a suggestion that creates clarity out of confusion or one that gives insight that's transformational. Your ideas are a reflection of who you are, how you think, what you feel, and what you've learned from your own experiences.

Willingness to share ideas is powerful. There is no way of assessing the impact we have on others by offering them our points of view. Each of us is unique. Our experiences are unique. Our perspectives are unique.

No one has traveled your road, been faced with your specific challenges, or possesses your knowledge. You are uniquely qualified to be you. Your ideas matter. There are times, however, when you could doubt yourself. You make a suggestion that someone else discounts. You share an idea you want to implement and the response is negative. Suddenly you feel self-conscious and unsure. It's unrealistic to think that every time we have something to say, our contribution will meet with unquestioned approval. Because we each differ, it's predictable that our points of view will also differ. The key is to recognize that you don't have to have agreements from others for your ideas to matter. They're important if for no other reason than they may help someone define what works for them.

Just as it's normal to be sensitive to another's negative response, it's also important to honor differing points of view. Everyone's ideas matter.

Whether we agree or not is irrelevant. We can't possibly know the thinking behind every idea. No one can know our thinking, either. All we can do in a sharing arena is listen, participate, evaluate, and allow the exchange from one to another to produce some action.

Never let your reaction to another's ideas or their reactions to yours diminish what you have to offer. Some ideas will fly and others will lay dormant. Some will appear well received and others will end up being dismissed. Your ideas have value not only because they reflect who you are, but also because they represent the gift you bring to others.

Choose your words with care. Share from an open heart. Be eager to listen and learn. Welcome feedback.

Remember, your ideas matter. They make a difference. You have no way of knowing when or where. Just know.

Show Up and Be Remembered

Woody Allen once said, "Seventy percent of success in life is just showing up." You've got to show up to be remembered!

How often have you resisted going somewhere but allowed a friend to talk you into going and ended up having a wonderful time? I'm amazed at stories I've heard of people meeting someone special at an event they at first declined.

My friend Hilda was resistant to being "fixed up" by a friend. As a 50-year-old divorcee, she was worn thin on having to get dressed and pretend to be totally excited about yet another blind date. So she said no to her friend Judy on several occasions.

Well, Hilda finally decided to get Judy off her back by saying yes to a double date with Judy and her husband. She thought that being with her friends would at least ease the pressure and make a typical date more comfortable. To her surprise, she had a lovely time. Her date, Lance, turned out to be quite nice and although he was visiting from out of state, he indicated an interest in coming back again to see her. The "double dating" went on a few times over three or four months.

Then one day, Hilda received a call from Lance. He said he wanted to visit again but without the "double date" scenario they had previously experienced. He was willing to stay at a nearby hotel to enjoy her company for the weekend.

Hilda was thrilled at the change of events and found herself excited about his visit. They had a wonderful few days together, not needing the facilitation of friends to make their time enjoyable. They eventually fell in love and several months later he moved in. Soon afterward, they announced their engagement and have been married more than eight years.

Another friend of mine, Sharron, met a guy through an Internet dating service and developed an on-line/telephone relationship with him. This lasted several weeks before they decided to meet. They spoke with ease, had much in common, and agreed to exchange photos before their actual first date. When my friend received her Internet man's photo, she became broken hearted. He was nothing like how she thought he'd look and began questioning herself whether she wanted to meet him because she found his "look" so unappealing. All she kept thinking was "how could someone so terrific look so ordinary?" Encouraged by friends and concluding "what's the big deal of one date" she said yes to their first date.

Sharron arrived a bit early and waited in the lobby of their selected restaurant. Moments later, a rather handsome man came up to her and introduced himself. He had recognized Sharron from her photo. She nearly fell over.

The picture of her date, David, looked nothing like the real thing! Over dinner, Sharron decided to share the uncertainty she had had after seeing the photo. She decided to ask him about the photo he'd sent, and why it looked so different from the real thing.

David told Sharron that when she asked him to exchange pictures, he couldn't find a current one, so he popped an old fraternity photo in the mail! The story would obviously have had a totally different ending if Sharron decided not to pursue a relationship based on one image. Sharron and David are now married.

See what can happen when you show up?

It's Best When You Don't Want To

The conclusion: The *best* time to show up is when you are feeling the most reluctant. Be willing to explore despite initial first impressions or judgments. Somehow the universe surprises us when we are caught off guard.

Showing up has two faces: physical and mental. Being physically present is the more obvious. Of course, you have to be somewhere to experience what that place has to offer.

More important than physical participation is mental involvement. It's easy to spot people who are physically present but mentally absent. They may be standing alone, faraway in thought, quiet and uninvolved.

In that same situation, one can spot others who are engaged in conversation, sharing ideas, connecting with friends, and creating new relationships. While both scenarios are played out everywhere, you can have the greatest impact on others when you show up and participate. We remember those who participate.

You are unique. You bring your special skills wherever you go. You determine your connection with your surroundings. You make a difference in other's lives because of all of your qualities and experiences.

Think of all the individuals you impact in a single day! When you express gratitude to people you meet, share an idea that can help someone else's progress, laugh at someone's joke, empathize during someone's setback, or make a phone call to a friend or colleague, you are not only "showing up," but you are also "being remembered" because you care. The operative word there is *care*.

As you think about life's playground, recognize how

important it is to the rest of us that you show up. The next time you decide not to show up, change your mind! You never know whom you might meet or who will benefit simply because you showed up and you were remembered.

Create Fulfillment in Your Life

"Those who have learned the power of sincere and selfless contribution experience life's deepest joy: true fulfillment."
— Anthony Robbins

When I think about all the "things" in my life, it becomes clear that materialism is no substitute for connecting yourself with a worthy cause, being with family, participating with people who share the same vision and values, or doing something for someone without expecting anything in return. The feeling of fullness you get because your heart is alive with energy and purpose is immeasurable.

There's no substitute for doing something about which you are passionate. We can experience fulfillment through volunteerism, connection with your spiritual self, working toward a far-reaching goal, being someone's support or mentor, or doing any activity that elevates your sense of self. It's worth both time and energy to search for and find that vehicle or outlet which reflects your uniqueness and values your participation.

Denis Waitley says, "Personal satisfaction is the most important ingredient of success." Feeling satisfied and knowing that who you are and what you do contributes to the well-being of people and community is powerful. Fulfillment is not the job you perform or the task you accomplish. Fulfillment is based on how you feel about yourself because of the difference "being you" makes!

So let me ask you: "Are your life's experiences relating to feeling fulfilled? Are you connected to something bigger than you? Are you engaged in tasks that are rewarding? Are you stretching your mind to explore new possibilities? Most importantly, are you willing to consider other options that could take you to a place you've not yet been?"

Take the time to expand your self-awareness. Find answers to these difficult questions. Congratulate yourself if you are leading a fulfilling life. Give yourself permission to seek more rewarding avenues if you're not. In either case, remember that life is a journey.

It's your journey. What you do and accomplish in this lifetime and who you share your life with are your choices. Everything is a choice.

Remember, you and your contributions matter!

The Joy of Connecting

Up Close and Personal: It's All About Connecting

Several years ago while vacationing with my husband in Branson, Missouri, I was feeling uneasy about what I was doing, the direction of my life (not ours together), and its purpose. We were sitting in a quiet, lovely dining room at the top of a hotel overlooking the city and the night lights. Before our vacation, I had been thinking about all the help I was offering others, and the relationships that were forming because I had made introductions. These introductions and relationships were producing significant results for others. I wondered when it was going to "come back to me" as the giver. I had been wanting to share these thoughts with Phil. Both this setting and our closeness offered an opportunity to be open with him.

I didn't want Phil to confuse feelings about my life with feelings about our marriage. I certainly didn't want him to think that I was dissatisfied with our marriage in any way. It was my personal journey that had me troubled.

What am I Supposed to be Doing?

Trusting both our relationship and Phil's ability to be a wonderful listener, I asked Phil to share what he thought my life purpose was. As usual, he didn't have any problem offering his comments.

"What you're *doing* is exactly what you're *supposed to be doing*," he said.

I just didn't get it. How can that be my life purpose? He told me that the way I connect with people leaves an *indelible imprint on people's souls*. I thought, "Wow, that's a wonderful thing to say! But what *do I do?*"

Phil continued. "You guide people. You mentor. You show people by your example how to care, appreciate, support, and love one another. I can't tell you what this will ultimately become for you someday, but I know that you must keep doing what you're doing because it's *who you are*. You are a leader. You teach people. You are an example of how to be for others. This *will* translate into something tangible. Be patient. It *will* happen. Others *will* want to learn from you."

This feedback was incredibly reassuring. While he couldn't give me the answer I was seeking, our conversation did offer me hope that someday the answer would come and that it would be the result of all that my life had reflected up to that time. I decided to just keep doing what I did so naturally and trust the future.

I could never have imagined that this reassuring conversation would lay the foundation for the grand plan of being a published author and guiding women through a *new way of being* for themselves and for each other. I could never have imagined that this would be the reward I had been seeking.

To be sharing this exact moment of time with you and to offer you my ideas through my own experience is an honor.

Doing is Not Being

I think that as women, we do "what we have to do" on automatic pilot because I think we are programmed that way. We get so caught up (understandably) in our day-to-day responsibilities that I wonder if we ever *take the time* to pursue our own dreams or even identify what they are!

I've come to recognize that *doing* is not *being*. The Eastern thinkers and philosophers always tell us, "Don't do. Be." Somewhere along the way, many of us got lost in diminishing our own value either because of the demands placed on us, or by choices that didn't best serve our interests.

As you know, I'm all about connecting. However, it took me a long time to recognize in myself what others saw in me. To find joy in connecting with others, you first have to find the joy in connecting with yourself. The joy comes when what you *do* is congruent with who you *are*.

If you love what you do, it's likely that you feel the same about who you are. You feel the possibilities of each day as it presents itself. You know you're making a difference in the world. You feel loved and appreciated. You *acknowledge* that your life has meaning and you feel fulfilled. When you are in this place, you eagerly connect with everyone. You want to be part of their lives, embrace their journeys, enrich them, and *be* enriched because connections create joy.

On the other hand, if you and the life you are leading are not congruent — guess what? You are still capable of making the changes necessary to be in alignment.

Sure, it requires work. Finding your life purpose and taking the steps to *live it* is not easy. It is, however, *essential* if you want to feel the joy of connecting. Understanding this principle reaps immeasurable rewards. Being connected with yourself is empowering. You'll feel so full and overflowing inside that you'll *want* to share who you are with others and you'll *want* them to share themselves with you. I know. I live in that place and I can tell you with certainty that the feeling is *compelling*.

You Are How You Act

Remember that everywhere you go, wonderful people surround you. They may be neighbors, colleagues, service workers, relatives, or casual acquaintances. During every encounter, you give off reliable indicators of how you are feeling, whether or not your life is joyful, and how much you value those who are with you at that moment. With each encounter, how you act and the ways in which you do or don't connect create those indicators.

Think about that. How much you engage deeply with others or how you choose to stay detached reflects how you feel about yourself. I love connecting at gasoline pumps, in line at the supermarket or at the bank, while browsing at the library, waiting to obtain a movie ticket, in a waiting room or anywhere. Just like my mother does! Even if we talk about the weather or someone's outfit, I simply enjoy having a conversation and making a connection. It's fun. It surprises others.

It feels good to acknowledge another's presence. Once you get into the habit of initiating a connection, you too will feel the joy of doing it. When you feel good about yourself and about your life, connecting happens naturally.

How Do You Feel About *You*?

Are you happy in your own skin? Are you pleased with how you look, the company you keep, the relationships you have, the work you do, the boundaries you maintain, and your spiritual life?

I'm not suggesting that everything has to be perfect for you to be ready to be a connector. However, I know that the more balanced you feel and the more purposeful your journey, the more you'll want to connect who you are with the world. You'll want to know what makes others tick, what's important to them, what they need, and how "who you are" can serve "who they are."

We're all headed in some direction that may or may not serve our highest good. Each one of us has a role to play in the complete human arena. Others benefit from you to the degree that you share your story — your values, ideas, skills, etc. — once you know where they are in their own plans.

Does this make sense? Think about it. You wouldn't expect a doctor to prescribe anything without first knowing where and what was troubling you. The same is true in relationships. It's joyful to plug into someone else's story and find ways to connect from your heart to theirs!

Yet It's Not About You

The connecting I'm describing is not about you. It's about the other person. Remember, when *you* are overflowing with self-love, you don't *need* to connect. You *want* to connect.

I learn so much when I engage others in talking about themselves. By their sharing who they are and what they do, it opens dialogue, creates interest, and brings joy to both parties. I don't *need* to tell what I do as much as I *want to know* what someone else is all about. When you lead with a genuine interest in someone else, *you* become memorable.

How different a paradigm this is than leading with, "This is who I am and this is what I need." For instance, at most networking events, the majority of people are eager to tell you about themselves, what they're selling, what they want. They're crying out, "Do business with *me.*" Are you eager to do that or would a conversation centered around mutual interests be more appealing?

I encourage you to let others lead first and to support their side of the conversation. If they ask about you, that's great. If not, it speaks miles about the other person's intention. Their intention is not to find out what *you* need, but rather, they want *you* to "do business with *them*." This is not a connection; it's a hidden agenda! On the other hand, when you show sincere interest in someone else, it will likely flow back to you as well. When you've been listening, it's likely the listener will offer, "I've told you a lot about me. What is it that *you* do?"

How Do You Start Connecting with Others?

As you think about being a connector, you're wondering, "How do I even get started?" The answer is just begin.

Begin in situations that are easy and casual. Simply engage in a conversation. Let someone know you admire what she's wearing. If you like her hairstyle, ask who does her hair. Be observant. Find something like a simple compliment that opens a door. By focusing on the other person, you are *showing* them they're being noticed.

When I finish a transaction at a cash register, instead of saying "Thank you," I replace the ordinary with "I appreciate you." What a different response that generates! Is there anyone who doesn't want to be appreciated? When we feel great from the inside out, we appreciate everyone and everything. It is simply part of the picture! As I've suggested before, it begins by first connecting with yourself. You love the world when you love who you are.

We all know unpleasant people. Believe me, I'll bet they're unhappy with their lives and the people in them.

Their hearts are so empty that they don't have the energy to give others the go-ahead. I think full hearts produce energy which when shared, cannot go unrecognized! Overflowing hearts love the joy of connecting. They do it effortlessly once they know the value to the recipient as well as to the giver.

People notice other people who are connectors. By effortlessly showing how to connect, you are demonstrating a way in which others can learn. Connecting reflects generosity. It's being in a giving spirit.

You can't give what you don't have. This comes back to the reality that individuals who are healthy givers have filled themselves up first. They can then share by offering support, caring, listening, and more. When people complain that they're *always* on the giving side and don't feel reciprocated, it's because they feel depleted. When we are connected with ourselves and *know* the value that comes from giving of ourselves, giving doesn't diminish us; it enriches us.

We deserve connection. If affirms us. It enriches us. It broadens our relationships. Experiencing the joy that comes from connecting is a natural high. It allows each of us to make a difference for someone else over and over again. People want to feel that their lives matter, that who *they are* matters. Connection fosters that feeling.

Patience Leads to Genuine Connections

I was asked to participate with several other women in a taping for a pilot television show featuring women. We were told that we'd each be interviewed for several minutes.

There were different time slots available so I registered for the 11 am to 1 pm time slot on a Saturday. When I arrived, I was immediately told to go to "makeup" where a professional would improve on the face I had put together. It was very exciting. I felt special, like I was in Hollywood!

When the makeup professional was finished, I hardly recognized myself. Then the waiting began. From 11 am to 4:30 pm, I waited in the restaurant where the taping was staged. Finally, it was my turn to be in the spotlight.

I kept thinking, "Why was I one of the last people to be taped?" I decided I wouldn't let it get me down. So I created energy by introducing myself and meeting every woman at the taping. I had a wonderful day. I found out how each person got invited and what they were going to talk about. I created some new relationships by using the time to connect instead of complain. Most of the women asked to be placed on my e-mail list for the next women's gathering at my home and also expressed interest in my book and its themes.

When it was *finally* my turn, the co-anchor was terrific. We spent a few minutes together and he expressed genuine interest in my book and ideas. The following day, on a Sunday, he sent me an e-mail saying that not only does he want my book, but he's inviting me back to do a segment.

Maybe going last was in my best interest. Based on a two-to-three minute interview, he told me, "Bonnie, I can learn a lot from you about listening and connecting!" He also remembered my patience throughout the whole process. I clearly turned a frustrating situation into one that produced huge results.

It's All About Connection

You show up and seize the opportunity to produce wonderful results. You simply allow others to benefit because of who you are. It's magic. It's powerful. When you are the initiator, it takes all of the pressure off of you.

Can you think of a reason *not* to be a connector? Everyone wants to connect. Everyone *is waiting* to connect. You have the skills and confidence to be that kind of person.

You can make a huge difference in people's lives by handing them the chance to communicate. You're also demonstrating a way of being that can inspire *them* to be a connector. You never, ever know where any connection, even if it seems insignificant, can lead. Had I been one of the first people to be filmed on that Saturday, I would've left early and totally lost out on all of the day's events. Yet, by making the choice to engage with the other women waiting their turns, my experience was memorable.

As you consider the places you frequent or the activities you participate in, why not take a pro-active role? Experience how it feels. Trust yourself. Go without an agenda other than connecting with those around you. Ask questions. Focus on listening. Be present.

I believe you'll be amazed at how you'll feel taking the lead rather than waiting for something to happen. You can do it: It's worth the effort to be the one who makes the difference for others.

Don't just *do* connection. *Be* a connector. It will change your life!

Future Connections

The journey began with 3,000 individuals. We all stood at the starting line for the Avon 3Day Walk knowing that we could not reach the finish line without that first important step. Three days later, we had connected through our energy, our commitment, our enthusiasm and our sweat. Through the joy of connecting with each other and those who could not find the strength to walk — like Deb and Marcia — we had created a supportive, caring and committed corps of people.

The Avon 3Day Walk was just a moment in time. Time moves on and so do our lives. The joy of connecting only comes when we continue to find ways and venues to create and recreate this feeling of support, caring, and commitment.

Like the Avon 3Day Walk, all things begin with a single step.

Walk In My Boots ~ The Joy of Connecting is my first step in growing the concept of professional women being with one another in a supportive environment.

The Joy of Connecting women's gatherings are already successful in Atlanta. It is my intention to create support groups for women entrepreneurs, business owners, and other professional women all over the country. By replicating this spirit in a simple format, participants will have the opportunity to introduce themselves and their businesses to one another. They can ask for what they need in the comfort of a safe and informal setting. During these memorable evenings, new relationships blossom both personally and professionally. The synergy of mutual support creates incredible results!

Eventually, The Joy of Connecting website will have chat rooms linked to www.bonnierossparker.com globally expanding this supportive environment. As our sisterhood grows, the gatherings and contact information will be posted on a continual basis.

Connecting is a reflection of loving ourselves, loving each other, and recognizing the role we all play in creating a global heart. Join me and walk in my boots to experience the magic. Make every connection count! After all, we are, indeed, one family.

About Bonnie Ross-Parker

Bonnie is a multi-dimensional businesswoman/entrepreneur with a background in education, franchise development, publishing, mentorship, network marketing, and community development. She combines vision with a unique set of skills. Formerly the Associate Publisher of *The Gazette Newspaper*/Atlanta, she focuses her energies on supporting women. She earned a Certification in Network Marketing at the University of Chicago and several of her articles on owning one's own business and entrepreneurship have appeared in publications including: *Wealth Building*, *Home Business Magazine*, *Business to Business* and *Entrepreneur's Business Start-Ups*. In 2002 Bonnie received The Athena Award — an honor designed to acknowledge women of leadership in cities throughout the United States. She is the author of *Walk In My Boots ~ The Joy of Connecting*. Bonnie lives in Atlanta with her Professional Speaker/Author husband, Phil. Referred to as *America's Connection Diva*, Bonnie's three grandsons call her "Nana Boots".

Connect with Bonnie @ 770-333-9028
bootgirl@bonnierossparker.com
www.bonnierossparker.com

Order Form

Walk In My Boots ~ The Joy of Connecting
by Bonnie Ross-Parker

Shipping Information

_____
NAME

_____
ADDRESS

_____
CITY   STATE   ZIP

_____
DAYTIME PHONE   E-MAIL

To order by mail, send check or money order to:

Bonnie Ross-Parker
1231 Bickham Way
Smyrna, GA 30080

770-333-9028
bootgirl@bonnierossparker.com

For office use only
Date _____
Filled _____
Shipped _____

Add $3 per book for shipping and handling.

COST	NO. OF COPIES	TOTAL
$16.95 US		
$22.00 CDN		

TOTAL REMITTED _____

Discount 10% for 5+ copies

Please indicate the name of the person to whom this book will be personalized.

_____
NAME